T0301198

THE BOUNDLESS RIVER

Mathijs Deen

THE BOUNDLESS RIVER

Stories from the Realm of the Rhine

Translated from the Dutch by
Jane Hedley-Prôle and Jonathan Reeder

MACLEHOSE PRESS
QUERCUS · LONDON

First published in the Netherlands as *De grenzeloze rivier* by
Thomas Rap in 2021

First published in Great Britain in 2024 by

MacLehose Press
An imprint of Quercus Editions Limited
Carmelite House
50 Victoria Embankment
London EC4Y ODZ

An Hachette UK company

The publisher gratefully acknowledges the support of
the Dutch Foundation for Literature

A CIP catalogue record for this book is available
from the British Library.

ISBN (HB) 978 1 52942 416 4
ISBN (TPB) 978 1 52942 418 8
ISBN (Ebook) 978 1 52942 419 5

10 9 8 7 6 5 4 3 2 1

Designed and typeset in Sabon by Libanus Press Ltd, Marlborough
Printed and bound in Great Britain by Clays Ltd, Elcograf S.p.A.

It is to be hoped that one day, a clever geologist with a literary bent will write a pleasing, accessible book about the history of the Rhine. It would contain much that is surprising.

Onze Groote Rivieren (*Our Great Rivers, 1938*),
Jacobus Thijsse

The Rhine was always there.

Kim Cohen, palaeogeographer

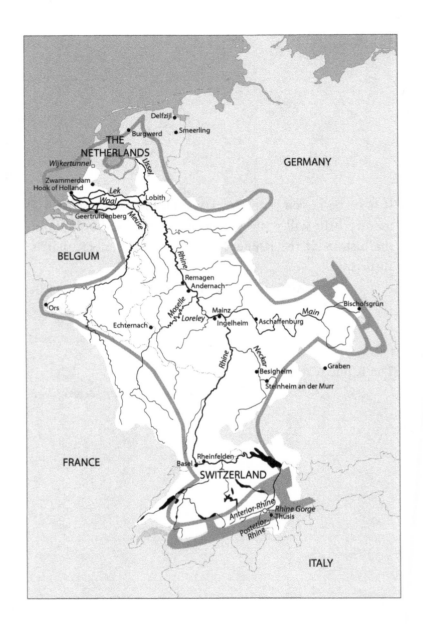

CONTENTS

PREFACE

It was Thursday 13 September, 2018, and on the Mediterranean islet of Vis, long tables had been laid overlooking the sea. Garlands with lanterns hung between the pine trees. The sun had set, there was an afterglow in the west.

My daughter was getting married and I was sitting opposite her. Ed, the man on my left, had just sat down after making a speech to the bridal couple. Besides being the British stepfather of my daughter, Ed is also a geologist. Glass in hand, he had begun with the observation that we were on an island in the Adriatic Sea about which lots of interesting geological things could be said, but that he would refrain, because that wasn't what we'd all come for. "Tonight, it's about the bride and groom," he reassured the guests.

What followed was an appropriately teasing speech leading up to the confession that, though he'd never said it in so many words, he loved my daughter and wished her every happiness in the world. "Not too bad," I said when he'd sat down again, in a lame attempt at British understatement. He grinned. Twenty years earlier he had married my ex-wife. Because of his work, he took her and my daughter over the sea to Scotland, and now we were sitting here. I'd made my speech to her earlier and people cried. When he spoke, people laughed.

"Say, speaking of geology . . ." I said, trying to get the conversation back on track, "I'm writing a book about the

Rhine. And now that we're talking about life events" – I nodded at the bridal couple – "suppose the river were a person . . ."

I was briefly distracted by my daughter, who had interpreted my nod as a greeting and was greeting me back, holding her wine glass aloft. As one man, Ed and I seized our glasses and raised them ceremoniously in her direction. She laughed, we laughed too.

"Supposing the river were a person," I continued, when my daughter's attention was diverted elsewhere, "then it would also be born and die." Ed nodded, put down his glass and looked at his plate.

"If the Rhine were a child, it would be a child of the Alps – because that's where its source is. But the Alps weren't always there. Tell me how they came into being. You know all about that kind of thing. Suppose we'd been able to witness it."

He looked up, his face earnest. It struck me how grey his hair had gone. I too was growing old, I knew, and the thought occurred to me that we were both guests of the next generation, that things come and go without you being able to stop them.

"Suppose time isn't an issue," I went on. "The Alps aren't there yet, we're standing on Europe's southern coast, we set a hypothetical clock – each minute is a million years – and we watch what's happening. What will we see? Do we see Italy sailing towards us till it crashes into the coast, and the mountains suddenly rise up under our feet?"

Ed shook his head, slid his plate aside and grabbed a napkin, which he smoothed flat on the table. "If it were just up to gravity," he said, "then we'd be living on a billiard ball."

I nodded, but he could see I didn't understand.

"The earth would tug at everything that stuck up, until its surface was totally flat," he explained.

I pictured land that was as level as the sea, water running off shin-high coasts as if from a saucer in the rain.

Meanwhile, Ed had positioned his hands on either side of his napkin. "Gravity isn't alone, though, there's another force at play," he said, "and that's continental drift. In the Eocene, Africa was on a collision course with Europe. And that's not over yet. Africa is still heading our way, and in the end it will shunt the Mediterranean out of existence. But back then, mini continents went ahead of the main landmass. Italy being one of them. A tiny chunk of Africa pushed out in advance of the troops."

I watched as his hands gradually moved towards each other. Because they were holding the edges of the napkin flat, the fabric in the middle began to bulge up.

"Look," he said, nodding at his right hand, "that's Italy . . ." and then at his left . . . "And this is Europe. That's how they drifted together. The seabed is heavy and sank downwards, so one continent began to slide over the other. That's how the Alps were pushed up, you see?"

He was looking anxiously at the napkin, at the ridge that was gradually rising up in the middle, centimetre by centimetre. It went well for a while, but then began to slump. Ed tried to shore up the collapsing mountain ridge, but without success. He seemed about to say more, but then gave up the attempt.

"It's a bit more complicated than that," he concluded.

He smoothed the napkin flat again and spread it over his lap. I looked past the bridal couple out to sea.

"But before Italy had even appeared on the horizon,

what would you have noticed first?" I persisted. "What would have been the very first sign of things to come?"

Ed shrugged. "Earthquakes, I reckon," he said.

"Tsunamis?" I asked.

"Very likely."

Then the meal was served.

Two days after the wedding, early in the morning, I took the ferry back to the mainland of Croatia. Halfway across, it grew light. The sky turned orange above the craggy mountain range on the horizon, rising up like a slowly advancing wall of surf a thousand metres long.

Fishing boats bobbed about, occasionally a dolphin's dorsal fin broke the surface. It was dead calm, the water as smooth as glass. Until a ripple passed across the entire expanse of the sea, no more than a foot or so high. After a while I realised that it was gradually moving from north-east to south-west.

Consulting my earthquake app, I saw there had been a tremor just off the coastal town of Šibenik, slightly north-east of Vis. There the sea was strewn with islets that stuck out of the water like miniature mountain peaks. The tremor hadn't registered more than 4.2 on the Richter scale: just enough to cause a ripple on the sea and a few scattered reports of creaking floors and a glass tumbling from a table's edge.

BIRTH

I dreamed that I was living slowly,
More slowly than an ancient stone –
A nightmare: above me, around me, below me
All shook, twitched, sprouted. I alone
was still.

From Time, *M. Vasalis*

Of course there was a one last day when nothing had yet happened. When the south of Europe was densely forested and the land, under its canopy of leaves, sloped down to the coast of a calm, nameless sea. There was no language, no-one to give things names. That happened only tens of millions of years later, when the distant descendants of the squirrel-like mammal Plesiadapis – still clambering around those European forests at the beginning of this story – had evolved into geologists. They learned that the continents, seemingly fixed in place, were actually loose floes floating around sluggishly – slower than a nail takes to grow – on deep vortices of molten rock.

The vanished sea that had lapped the southern coast of Europe was retroactively named the Valais Ocean. Banana-shaped, it was connected to the Atlantic Ocean in the west by a broad strait. To the east, its bed gradually shelved upwards to create a paradise of scattered coral islands in clear, shallow water. Yet further east lay the Tethys Ocean which, widening like a funnel, branched into the Panthalassa, a melancholy, desolate superocean that encircled all the continents.

Though the name suggests otherwise, the Valais Ocean was an inland sea. That was not apparent on Europe's southern coast, of course, except for the fact that week-old storms, bouncing off distant, encircling coasts, could suddenly return like ghosts in the form of waves coming out of nowhere during spells of calm weather. But it typically resembled a sea coast: water stretching to the horizon and a line of surf rolling back and forth. The slight tide refreshed the water in the rock pools, where birds and other predators hunted gobies, sea urchins, crabs and shrimps.

When it rained on the forests, filling the rivers, the deltas would spew sand that spread out in the sea like cloudy fans, extending for hundreds of kilometres. And sometimes, if the rain poured down with such force that the rivers burst their banks, engulfing parts of the forest, they didn't just sweep sand to the sea, but pebbles and uprooted trees as well. Days later, the tree trunks would wash onto the beach. Sometimes entire shoals of fish would be buried under avalanches of river-borne sand. They died, and were gradually buried deeper and deeper under the river's sediment.

In calm weather, the sea was crystal clear and warm; close to the shore, large shoals of fish washed calmly back and forth with the movement of the waves. The sea stretched to the horizon, though on clear days you might have spotted clouds gathering on the skyline, as if over distant, sun-warmed land. Land that, at the end of a hot day, chased the sea breeze so high into the sky that it condensed into thunderclouds. During the pitch-black nights there would be flashes of lightning, but too far off to result in thunder.

This was in the middle of the Eocene, more than forty million years ago, and the summer was endless. Where Stuttgart now stands, there were whispering treetops and surf. Where Switzerland is, was only sea.

Dinosaurs had vanished twenty million years earlier – except for the birds, that is, who had recovered well from the impact of the big meteorite. They swarmed above the treetops as evening fell, or foraged along the shoreline. It wasn't clear from their shape whether the predatory mammals they flew away from would develop into cats, wolves, martens or bears.

*

You could claim that these were the first signs: the clouds on the horizon that, like heralds kitted out with lightning bolts, announced the arrival of something bigger. But it's more likely that one day, the ground emitted a deep, protracted groan. That the earth trembled, the trees in the forest swept back and forth, and that the sea suddenly retreated from the land. Birds flocked to the mud flats, where surprised fish lay stranded, flapping their tails and gasping. The feast was short-lived, because at the horizon the sea turned, rushed up the sharply shelving ocean floor and poured onto the land. It knocked down trees, pushed water back into the rivers, hurled shoals of fish onto the forest floor and spread out, only retreating days later. The tsunami had left havoc in its wake. It would take years for the forest to recover. But that didn't matter – there were years aplenty.

Recalling what had happened, the survivors avoided the tideline for a while, then produced young that did not comprehend their fear. Soon, everything was as before. Until the next earthquake.

There was something going on at sea, or rather: there was something going on *under* the sea. But nothing that an unwitting coastal resident would notice. For a bird, an islet off the coast is a place to land; for a tree, a place to take root. The fact that the islet wasn't there a few thousand years ago, and that it's grown a few hectares in size in the last thousand years, represents a change too gradual to affect mere mortals. In the intervals between earthquakes, the animals of the Eocene couldn't know that they lived in turbulent times. Because the Earth's heartbeat is infinitely slower than that of her lodgers.

The Mediterranean's a pigsty.

Douwe van Hinsbergen

Mountains are like waves with an abundance of time. They rise out of the earth, climb to their highest point and then sink down again. Their rolling stones are like water droplets, their avalanches like foam.

Suppose we're standing on the coast and time speeds up. The sun goes round and round like a sock in a spin dryer, faster and faster, until there isn't a sock anymore, just a streak. Day and night merge into the twilight of an overcast afternoon, the winds from every compass point cancel each other out. Changes in the weather, changes in season disappear. Everything you would normally seek shelter from falls away, and we're standing in a becalmed, soundless world in which the Earth, rather than the sea, seems to have become liquid.

We look out to sea, a cloudy mirror radiating muted light. It's not clear where the light is coming from.

A man joins us in this thought experiment. His name is Douwe van Hinsbergen. Like me, he comes from the east of the country. From Eibergen, to be precise, which, though this translates as "egg mountains", is as flat as a pancake. He left his hometown in search of mountains and became professor of geology at Utrecht University. And now we're standing here, looking southwards. Tens of thousands of years fly past, but still there's nothing to be seen.

"The Mediterranean's a pigsty," he says. "You can't see

it because it's covered by water. But underneath, everything's shifting around, all higgledy-piggledy. It's a right old mess."

For Van Hinsbergen, a sea isn't water but the crust that lies beneath the surface. As he sees it, Europe doesn't stop at the beach. She carries on as the seabed, stretching far southwards, to where a piece that's broken off the African continent is heading towards her like an advance messenger. A big chunk of the continental crust that will, in time, push up against Europe in the form of Italy. But for the moment it's still on its way and Europe is stooping to receive it. Her stony bottom sinks, allowing it to mount her slowly, centimetre by centimetre. She lets herself be pushed down further by its weight, into the hot depths, the treacly mantle below, where she goes limp, bending, twisting and writhing. Italy forces itself onto her, scrapes over her, scouring the rock from her bent back, raising it to the surface, propelling it forwards.

For now, Italy remains submerged, while these scrapings of Europe rise up out of the sea. At first they look like islands. But gradually they morph into a long strip of land being shunted towards the coast.

Douwe points towards the horizon and indeed small dark tufts have risen out of the sea, as if the weather's about to change. "Those are the Alps," he says. "They're still low, but they're on their way."

The ground beneath our feet has become restless, it billows slowly up and down, and here and there cracks appear in the surface. Europe's bowels tremble, and open to what's about to come.

To our right, on the distant horizon, the mountain ranges of the Vosges and the Black Forest rip apart and a trench opens up between them, growing deeper and deeper, until rubble and landslides hurtle down from the exposed cliff faces. Fire jets out of the rim of the trench, volcanoes pop up like molehills, spew lava, sputter and collapse back into the earth.

They're hell-raisers with short lives.

"Keep watching," says Van Hinsbergen. I look south again. In the few minutes that I've been distracted, the dark tufts on the horizon have swelled into a tsunami more than a thousand metres high, blotting out the horizon from west to east. The ground under our feet is buffeted this way and that, splitting apart in places as rocks shoot up out of the soil.

It's strange how this all happens in silence, except for a deep hum coming from beneath the earth, a tremor we feel rather than hear. The sea between us and the advancing mountains has grown narrow, a strange tension grips the land, as if Italy is hurrying now and Europe is bracing herself. The earth shakes and landslides crash into the sea to re-emerge as islets. Then, as if something has been consummated, a noise comes from deep under the ground – it sounds like a long sigh – and everything relaxes.

"Europe has broken off," Van Hinsbergen says. "Italy pushed her down so far that in the depths, the southernmost tip of the tectonic plate has snapped off. Now she can surface, just you watch . . ."

We're gradually lifted up, it's as if Europe is wrestling herself free from Italy and rising, centimetre by centimetre. What remained of the sea at our feet disappears, the seabed comes up, as slowly as a cork through treacle. The water runs off, evaporates. We're no longer standing on the coast, but at the foot of the mountains.

We gaze up at the rocks that have been boiled, flattened and folded under the sea, and then thrust upwards in a jumbled mass, looming into the sky.

"I told you," says Van Hinsbergen. "It's a pigsty."

Clouds have gathered above us, their route to the south cut off by the new barrier of stone. The world around us has grown colder, the tops of the mountains turn white and the ground becomes sodden. All the water that used to fall here and flow south into the sea now has to detour northwards, first collecting in an evaporating inland sea, then seeking its way across the plains, en route to a delta.

*

When the Alps were bulldozed into Europe, water and rubble continued to rain down from their northern slopes for millions of years. The debris cascaded into a sea arm, blocking off its western passage to the open sea. Its bed rose centimetre by centimetre, the water grew brackish, islands crept upwards and eventually there was nothing left along the northern foot of the Alps but scattered lakes, connected by a river: the Danube. In the thirty million years that followed, the Alpine Rhine flowed into this river, then headed for the Black Sea. But when barriers arose – the land was in constant flux – it left the Danube and sought a path westwards to the Rhône and the Mediterranean. It wasn't until around three million years ago that it found its current route northwards, joining a rain-fed river between the Rhenish Massif and the North Sea: the Proto-Rhine. Its course was more or less where the middle and lower reaches of the Rhine are today. Hungry for water, it had been busy extending its basin southwards for some time.

No-one knows exactly when the Alpine Rhine left the Rhône. But a day came when water from the Alps first found its way northwards. It joined the Proto-Rhine, causing it to swell unstoppably. The water level around the Lorelei rose and the current quickened, ripping off bushes, flooding pebble islands, uprooting trees that had grown on sandbanks for centuries and sending them floating northwards. There, in the flat region between mountains and sea, the Rhine burst its banks, cut off bends and overran the Roerslenk plain. Extending ever further beyond its bed – now far too narrow – it sought a way to the North Sea.

With redoubled strength, the water forced its way right into the delta. Whereas the gentle Proto-Rhine had carried only small particles of clay this far downstream, depositing them on the banks over the centuries, the violent, swollen Rhine swept millions of cubic metres of coarse sand and pebbles along with it. Traces of this sudden switch from clay to sand can still clearly be seen in the quarry pits of the Roerslenk, the Rhine's old course. The mineral composition of deep boreholes in the old river valleys show, too, that the Alpine grit reached our regions almost from one day to the next.

Back then, Europe was just entering an era of alternating ice ages and warmer periods. During the latter, forests shot up. The trees held the soil together, copious rain filled the Rhine with clear water, and – as the sea level rose and the coast shifted – the river carved out a bed for itself far inland. Because there was so little sediment in the water, the river hardly silted up. The rain over the Alps soaked loose unstable minerals like hornblende and epidote, fine grains of which were scattered on the banks downstream.

But when the ice ages arrived, the forests thinned out. Trees died and made way for steppe landscape. Glaciers cracked paths through the young mountains: the Alps, the

High Vosges and the southern Black Forest. Valleys were carved out, rocks split off, and the water, milky white with sand and clay, raised its banks. The river created immense plains in its delta. The sea level sank and the Rhine strayed further and further north, flowing through its own sediment and over the exposed seabed.

RIVERBEDS

Nature provided well for our defence,
setting the Alps as a shield
between us and the German madness.

From Italia mia, benché 'l parlar
sia indarno, *Petrarch*

During a geography lesson in my final year of primary school, our teacher, standing in front of a big map of Europe, told us that if you followed the Rhine far enough upstream, you'd eventually reach a spot where it was so narrow you could jump over it.

It's an image I've never forgotten. Not because the Rhine played an important role in my life, on the contrary. I grew up in Twente, a landscape of little streams and woodland lakes. I only ever saw the Rhine from the back seat of the car, on the rare occasions that my parents happened to drive through the Dutch river region.

The reason it stuck, this image of a leap across the Rhine, was because the teacher was a sadist whose idea of fun was to take his pupils to the sandy playground and make them do long jump into the thorny bushes along its edge (in full view of the headmaster). He would place the board from which we had to launch ourselves about four feet from the bushes and spur us on. If you refused, he would pinch your cheek or twist your ear. Sometimes he would grab a boy by the armpits and knees, fold him double and stuff him into a waste-paper basket.

Forty-six years on, I haven't forgotten this as I cross the Rheinquellstrasse into the valley where the Posterior Rhine tumbles straight down from the mountain. It's mid-November, it has snowed, but the sky is a clear blue. The wind gusting

33

down the valley towards me comes from the glacier and is icy cold. Upstream, just in front of the snowy peaks that wall off the valley in the distance, the mountain stream curves gently to the right and disappears from view. Even though I'm only a few kilometres from its source, here, too, the Rhine has been corralled and tamed. The banks have been straightened and reinforced with large oblong boulders.

The Posterior Rhine is one of two mountain rivers in the Swiss canton of Graubünden that can claim to lead upstream to the source of the Rhine. At Reichenau, the Posterior Rhine flows into the Anterior Rhine, which springs from various mountain lakes further west, near the Oberalp Pass. At the Tomasee, the lake which lies furthest from the mouth of the Rhine (measured along the water), a sign is attached to a rock stating that this is the *Rheinquelle* – the source of the Rhine – and that the river runs for 1,320 kilometres before emptying into the sea.

The Tomasee might lie furthest from the Rhine's mouth at the Hook of Holland, but the Posterior Rhine with its tributaries branches furthest south of the entire river basin. Some of the rain that feeds it even comes from Italian mountains in the province of Sondrio, flowing into it via the Reno di Lei and the Avers Rhine.

I'm heading for the spot where the Posterior Rhine is so narrow that I can jump over it. At the valley entrance is a sign with a lot of information, but the wind is so icy I don't want to stop to read it. As I pass, I see a map and a reassuring little green light from which I conclude not only that it's okay for me to continue, but also that there are times when apparently it isn't. There are barrier arms too, but they're raised. A long concrete building, a shed of some kind, flanks the entrance to the funnel-shaped valley. A Swiss flag flutters above the flat roof.

Level with the entrance there is a little bridge across the river, which I cross, prompted by an instinct to steer clear of the shed and the flag.

I soon realise that I'm in some military training area where there's regular firing practice, as if the Swiss want to make it clear to the Rhine, even in its cradle, that it should keep a low profile.

After a kilometre, the artificial banks disappear and the riverbed fans out into a plain of weathered boulders that fills half the valley. The military road of flattened gravel that briefly ran high above the bank, like a dyke, has been replaced by levelled-off heaps of rubble in which heavy doors have been inserted, perhaps because military equipment is stored in them. There are also structures that can run on rails – I assume so that tanks can fire at them.

It's harder to make headway now that the caterpillar tracks have ended, the valley has narrowed and the artificial banks have made way for the natural jumble of fallen boulders and rocks worn smooth by water. I leap from stone to stone and clamber over the debris left by recent avalanches. The Rhine is still too wide to jump across. The boulders lying in and next to the river wear shiny hats of ice. On either side the mountains rise steeply. The waterfalls have been frozen into chandeliers of ice piled up to the sky.

The deeper I go into the valley, the more unexploded ordnance I find scattered among the rocks. I have to watch where I put my feet. But the afternoon is advancing, soon it will be dusk, and I'll be scrambling for a few more hours before I see the Rhine dwindle into trickles of water that disappear under the ice. I peer along the little river with the inexperience of a Lowlander, searching for a spot where I can jump. But where the river narrows, the current speeds up. And where the stream widens and the water flows more slowly, the boulders sticking through the surface are spaced too far apart and really slippery. For a kilometre now, I've seen no more unexploded ordnance, only fox scats on rocks and the hoofprints of chamois in the snow.

When at last the river is narrow enough to venture a crossing and I've decided, rather unheroically, to clamber instead of jump, and I've crossed the Rhine on my hands and feet in three slippery steps, I imagine how silly it must have looked, but it doesn't matter, there was no-one to see it. I kneel in the snow and drink from the Rhine; it tastes of stone.

When I leave the valley, now with the wind at my back and warmed-up limbs, I see on the information sign that I've been in forbidden territory, that the unexploded ordnance is potentially lethal, and that if something had happened to me it would have been entirely my fault.

What do you mean, the source of the Rhine
is in the Alps?

Kim Cohen, palaeogeographer

All of a sudden, Kim Cohen blows his top. We've been having a long chat about the genesis of Europe's landscape, about how rivers feel their way, about sinking trenches and rising mountain ranges. But when I tell him I've been to the Alps to see the source of the Rhine, he looks really cross.

"What do you mean, the source of the Rhine is in the Alps?" he says. "What a load of nineteenth-century baloney!"

"Well, without the Alps no Rhine, right?" I venture.

This doesn't make things any better. Cohen seems to swell in size. "This really gets my goat!" he says.

We're sitting in a windowless room that suddenly feels very small and oppressive. It's a conference room in the geoscience building of Utrecht University. Cohen, a palaeo-geographer, stares at the ceiling, searching for a way to tell me just how wrong-headed I am about the Rhine without scaring me too much. Then insight seems to strike. He lowers his gaze, looks at me and says emphatically, "The Rhine was always there."

He gets up and starts to sketch on a whiteboard. "The water in the Rhine doesn't just come from the Alps," he says. "A river isn't the same thing as its bed. People think that, but it's a misconception. A river is water, a sausage of water, yes . . . a sausage of water." He repeats the words under his breath, not dissatisfied with his metaphor. "And that water flows from the entire catchment area to the riverbed.

From the Black Forest, from the Vosges, from the Eiffel, from the Hunsrück."

He turns to face me.

"Just following the Rhine up the Alps until you find a little stream in the snow doesn't mean you understand the river. It's entirely random that you opted to be there and not upstream of the Moselle, the Neckar, the Lahn or the Main. It's a nineteenth-century *idée fixe* that to get the measure of a river, you have to reach its furthest point."

I listen silently, and his anger subsides.

"Because a river is also the water you *don't* see," he says, sitting down. "It's the groundwater between the beds, the water beside the lower reaches. A river doesn't stop at its banks."

"Isn't it just about names?" I hazard. "Up to the Alps the river is called the Rhine, after all, and the Moselle is called the Moselle. And the source of the Moselle . . ."

". . . is also a source of the Rhine," Cohen adds. "As is the rainwater in the Netherlands." He shakes his head. "Water doesn't have borders or a fixed location. Not so long ago there was a journalist here who said that the Rhine disappears into the Waal, the IJssel and the Lek." He gazes at me intensely. "But if so, where has the Rhine suddenly gone?"

*

Back then in that oppressive little room, I was taken aback by Cohen's annoyance. But later I came to understand it. When the Alps reached their present height during the Miocene, the Proto-Rhine – which discharged into the North Sea to the north-west – was already many millions of years old. But between the basin of the Proto-Rhine and the water that came from the Alps lay hundreds of kilometres of restless terrain, where mountains rose and trenches sank ever deeper into the ground. The remains of the supercontinent Pangaea were still breaking apart, the land was in flux. A trench appeared along the fault line running from Roermond to Cologne, and was used by the Proto-Rhine as a bed. Meanwhile the Ardennes, the Eiffel, the central mountain ranges of Germany: Taunus, Hunsrück and Sauerland – which collectively form the Rhenish Slate Plateau – were pushed up by the forces tugging the continent this way and that. To keep their courses, the rivers had to dig themselves deeper into their beds, centimetre by centimetre. You can still see from the meanders of the Moselle, the Lahn and the Sieg – three Rhine tributaries that drain the slate mountain region – that they came into being in flatter circumstances. As the ground around and under their beds was very gradually pushed up, perhaps only a few centimetres every century, they dug out their serpentine courses. New little tributaries streamed down from rising mountains.

A river's course is always provisional. Like a snake slithering imperceptibly slowly, it looks for the path of least resistance and greatest difference in gradient. The climate changes, the landscape changes, the river adapts. The water carries sediment, depositing it where it slows down. Sometimes a bed silts up, as if the river were getting in its own way. Then the water hesitates and looks for alternative routes.

Sometimes bends erode on the outside, banks crumble away and meanders find shortcuts. And if a river meets another river in its search, the course with the least resistance will capture the other's water. It's called beheading. So it can happen that a river that first discharged into the

Mediterranean alters its course for the North Sea, simply because while seeking lower ground it met a river flowing northwards, and it was easier to drain into that.

In this way the Proto-Rhine captured the Moselle from the Meuse and the Main from the Rhône. Even before the Alpine water had made contact with the Proto-Rhine, it was swollen with all the rain-fed rivers it had seized. It stretched its arms further and further southwards, towards the German mountains, where it carved out the picturesque Rhine Gorge.

The Lorelei, the high rock nestled in a tight bend of the river, was already there, looking more or less as it does now. Just with less water.

The Rhine was always there.

A HIPPOPOTAMUS

Three million years ago, an Atlantic salmon left her hunting grounds in the Northern Ocean and headed south, back to the river of her youth, to spawn. She was alone, big enough to handle the river, sure of her course. The Earth pulled at her, very weakly, she swam against its tug.

That's what she wanted: to go against the flow.

On her journey south, with the shimmering daylight above her and the black of the deep sea beneath her, everything went smoothly. When she swam into the North Sea from the ocean she tasted the first rivers, thin veils from distant estuaries. Nothing was familiar to her, she swam on.

Then came her first flash of recognition – the scent and taste of her own river: a few minuscule, floating grains of sediment, a hint of humic acid, somewhere in the cloudy fan unfolding into the seawater from the east. She lost interest in the Earth's pull, focusing instead on the unmistakable traces of her own river, very faint still, in the gentle current spreading out into the sea.

She whipped her tail and altered course upstream, towards water that grew ever murkier, against a strengthening countercurrent, the water first brackish, then fresh, her nose full of all kinds of tastes.

It was as if something was wrapped around her, a cocoon, protecting her against the fresh water. She thrashed hard against the current when it pushed her back and the water became shallow and erratic, stones scraping her belly, tailfin in the air; she fought and fought. She leapt, she flew, bears tried to swat her onto the bank, danger was everywhere but she kept going, because with every beat of her tail the trace of that one river grew a little stronger. There, in that dizzying sensory cocktail, was the taste of her youth, becoming ever more distinct as she fought her way upstream.

That's how she found the estuary, the river, the fork, the spot in the upper reaches that she'd imprinted in herself as a young fish. The place where she'd squirmed out of her egg six years previously. Everything tasted, smelled and felt as it had then, especially when it rained and forest soil washed into the river from the banks: the unique flavour of the stream of her birth. She was emaciated, she was exhausted, but she was home.

She picked up little pebbles with her mouth and slung them aside, gradually clearing out a nest in which she deposited her roe. A few thousand eggs in a shallow pit. Father, born and raised a bit further down the river, had shot his sperm over them and then, tired of life, allowed himself to be carried away downstream. For a few weeks more she had brushed sediment from the eggs with her tail and wafted oxygen-rich water over them. She hung above her brood like a Zeppelin, one and a half metres of shade, her dorsal fin sticking above the surface.

Then she too left, weary, thin as a bone. A wintry sun broke through, lighting up the clutch of eggs.

This happened three million years ago, just before the Alpine Rhine found the Proto-Rhine and the river took on its current form. The summers were still hot, and the winters mild. From the southernmost branches of the Proto-Rhine and the northernmost bend of the Alpine Rhine – still separate, but close – forests stretched away in every direction. Mastodons and rhinoceroses lumbered between the trees, ripping leaves from branches. Macaques and howler monkeys screeched in the canopies. Hippopotamuses bobbed in the river.

There was little to show that change was imminent. That winter, snow fell on the mountains of the Black Forest and the Vosges for the first time in hundreds of thousands of years. And when spring arrived, it took a long time to melt. The water that came down was chilly, but posed no threat to the salmon eggs, which thrive in cold temperatures. The river ran clear, the roots of the trees on the banks held on to most of the sediment. It was only during lengthy downpours that forest soil was washed into the water and it grew cloudy for a while.

The Proto-Rhine would soon be no more. When the wind was from the south, the mastodons that came down to the banks in the evening to drink could already smell the other river. They stuck their trunks in the air, sniffed, shook their heads, waded into the water, drank. What they smelled was the scent of the advancing Alpine Rhine, extending its course further and further northwards: grit, gravel, splintered rock, ice. The world cooled down, winters piled more snow on the mountaintops and every spring the meltwater coursed down the Alps with a bit more force than it had the previous year. The streams sought out one another, joined forces, meandered, strayed, carved out circuitous paths on their journey to the Belfort Gap, flat terrain between the Vosges and Jura mountains, behind which the Valley of the Rhône lay. The water was greenish white, milky and – in spring – raging. Boulders rolled, uprooted trees were swept along, got caught on rocks, collected branches and carcasses.

But this spring, all is still serene at the salmon's nest. The eggs have hatched. A swarm of small fry hangs above the nest, wriggling in the current. Chubby-bellied little creatures with tiny tails, sheltering between the pebbles. Drawing nourishment from their yolk sacs, they prey on flies and water fleas. They savour the water, imprinting its taste.

Life is just as it was six years ago for their father and mother; surviving, squabbling with siblings, hunting small water creatures and hiding – first from great crested newts, then from kingfishers, herons, perch, otters and bears – until, two years later, during a downpour, the few survivors of the nest let themselves be carried downstream on their first big voyage, to the sea. The water is cloudy and that is reassuring, because it means that predatory fish can see them only as brief silver flashes, tiny sunbeams. There were thousands of them when they hatched, fewer than ten have survived the two years in the river. Now they head off, not in a shoal, but each striking out on their own, leaving the nest, leaving the upper reaches of their own branch of the Proto-Rhine. An otter glides through the water, sees one shoot past, lunges, misses, watches her disappear into a rapid.

Sometimes the current almost comes to a standstill in deep pools, or swirls round in circles, gradually picking up speed again after a burst of rain. The banks grow further apart, strange savours come from all directions. The scent of the nest grows fainter, the river pushes and pulls, shadows of enormous fish hang in the water or loom up out of the depths.

On and on the young salmon swims, until the current slackens and a perplexing new taste pushes against the river. The water seems to falter, the river splits into branches and then sandbanks push up from below, blocking the way. She

48

hesitates at the threshold of another world, searching the bends of the delta until she finds an estuary and the sand retreats into the depths. The banks disappear, the water is salty and from somewhere below she feels a faint tug, even fainter than the fading traces of her own river's flavour. Now and then she still scents a whiff of home, a grain of sediment that has come along for the ride. But it's time to say farewell. She thrashes her tail, disappears northwards.

During her absence, the river she's left behind – whose scents and savours she's imprinted for her return journey – will change radically. The winter is colder than usual, and the spring that follows is violent. The Alpine snow melts, the tangle of riverbeds that have drained the water to the Rhône for the last few million years can no longer cope with the surge. The current, pushed back by the water that has accumulated, falters, then rushes northwards. It rips out trees and carries them along. Here and there they get stuck, blocking the river's path, making it climb, burst its banks, wash away woodlands, put wild animals to flight.

At the northernmost point, an arm of the river strays across the old watershed line and gets lost in the basin of the Proto-Rhine. Where brambles and ferns grew, a torrent of dirty ice water now seeks a path. Bears' dens flood, deer swim between the trees, a wildcat bolts up a tree, wraps itself around a branch and stares downwards. The forest floor has become a swirling lake; its waters, seeking lower ground, gush into the bed of a stream that flows into the river where the salmon was born.

Thus the Alpine Rhine found its way to the upper reaches of the Proto-Rhine. The mass of water that had built up a few days earlier, trying to enter the Rhône, felt the pull of the alternative route and began, at first slowly, then ever faster, to flow from west to north. Like a dam gradually crumbling, the watershed let more and more water past, and in the years that followed the Rhine swelled. The river became forceful, filling the flatlands between the Black Forest and the Vosges, further eroding the valley below the Lorelei and spreading itself over the swamps and plains of the delta until it reached the coast.

The Proto-Rhine, that tranquil, friendly river, had ceased to exist, and the Rhine as we now know it was born. It had become angrier, broader, cloudier, colder and more bitter. Coarser grains floated in the water. Levees grew along the banks, sand dunes heaped themselves up. At high water, the current carried whole pebbles all the way to the sea, the delta expanded. The fan of fresh water spread further than ever offshore.

All this time, our salmon was in the northern Atlantic. She hunted fish and shrimps off the Faroe Islands and grew quickly. After two years she saw other salmon leave, but she herself remained. Because she'd been born so far upstream, further than those others, she needed more time to build up the strength and body fat needed to tackle the long voyage home.

Although innately able to swim against the current and return to the exact river bend where she'd been born, she wasn't well equipped to handle change and unpredictable situations.

When she set off on her return journey after three years of hunting at sea, she swam purposefully, as her mother had. A big fish, one and a half metres long, yet no more than a dot in the ocean, floating weightlessly above the geomagnetic field, heading for the estuary, the gateway, the battle against the current. She swam slowly at night, more vigorously during the day, always on her guard. She no longer hunted, her appetite had made way for an all-consuming longing for the taste of home. She swam, she tasted, she sniffed, she sought, she anticipated. There was nothing else.

*

Had the salmon been a human – that's to say a thin-skinned loner attached to their personal routines and unable to cope with change – then this journey home would have sparked melancholy, confusion, anger and fear. The emotions a homesick person would feel upon returning to the city of their youth after a long absence, only to find it bombed to smithereens.

But the salmon isn't human, and her unblinking eyes and taut body betray no emotion. Unless it be the hesitation, the inner conflict of impulses that cause her to hang motionless in the estuary of the new Rhine. Although she vaguely recognises the taste of her own river, it's like an association that keeps eluding her. Driven out by a dominant cocktail of new, unfamiliar smells and savours. The river's current pushes her back towards the sea, she swims on, turns back, tastes, seeks. Fear wrestles with desire, other fish hesitate too. A sturgeon swims against the current beneath her, close to the estuary bed. She hangs motionless, watches.

Then swims on too.

Weeks pass, the days grow shorter, she swims against the current, which is much stronger than she's equipped to handle. She seeks out the inner bends, where the flow is weaker. There's a lot of water, an awful lot of water. Water full of strange tastes, in which the taste of her own river gradually grows stronger. But when, after journeying for six months, she reaches the spot where her rivulet once branched off, there's nothing that she recognises. The bend isn't there anymore, the banks have been washed away, the taste is diluted. Chilly, bitter water thunders past from a direction she doesn't understand, which she didn't even know existed. As if her home – where she thought she knew every nook and cranny – suddenly features a portal, a door she had never noticed before, thrown open wide, revealing a giant chamber full of banks, pools, rapids and whirlpools.

She has come so far, one of the very few to make it. Now she hangs in the current, lost. After a while she swims through the open portal, continuing upstream. The taste of her own river has suddenly disappeared. The water is cool and there are no other salmon, except for one small male, the kind that don't go to sea but disguise themselves as trout and stay in the river. He follows her. She swims against the new water, wriggles between the stones.

Four huge legs stomp around her, a hippopotamus sticks his head under the surface. Startled, she swims on, finds a tree trunk that has rolled a hollow in the gravel. She lies down and surrenders herself, deposits her eggs, pushes off and is carried away by the stream. She no longer resists.

Downstream, a bear swats her out of the water, crunches her head, sucks her poor perplexed brains from her frail skull. She thrashes her tail one last time.

A hippo's teeth,
I get carried away when I see them,
always find myself lost for words . . .

Kommer Tanis, North Sea fisherman

At the estuary mouths of the Rhine delta where, three million years ago, the puzzled salmon lingered, waiting for inspiration, fish still wait for an opportunity to swim up the river. Not because its taste or character has changed, but because it's been tamed and the routes are blocked. The Rhine discharges most of its water via the Nieuwe Waterweg ship canal and the Haringvliet estuary, the rest via the IJssel and the North Sea Canal. The Nieuwe Waterweg is the only route that's nearly always fully open; elsewhere dams, dykes and sluices bar the way to the spawning grounds.

And so the fish have to loiter outside the sluices of the Haringvliet, the North Sea Canal, and the Afsluitdijk – the huge dam between the Zuiderzee and the North Sea. Waiting for the navigation locks to open, or for the tide in front of the lock to turn and the current to weaken. Then off they go. Officials from Rijkswaterstaat – the executive agency of the Ministry of Infrastructure and Water Management – sometimes fish just outside the closed-off estuaries to see who's in the queue: houting, twaite, shad, smelt, flounder, sea lamprey, allis shad, elver, stickleback, sea trout and yes, salmon.

I'm heading for the tiny hamlet of Havenhoofd at the tip of Goeree, a delta island just south of Rotterdam, on my way to see Kommer Tanis, a North Sea fisherman until he lost his job and his trawler when the fishing fleet was cut back.

At low tide, almost a third of the Rhine's water, together

with two thirds of that of the Meuse, gushes into the sea just below the Haringvliet Dam. If the rivers are full, that can amount to twenty-five million litres a second. When the locks open, the fresh water churns and foams into the sea, forcing back the salt water. As the tide rises and the water has less far to fall, the turbulence dies down and the water grows calm. The sea pushes back towards the dyke. The sluice gates descend, the estuary is locked once again.

At least, that's how it was back when Kommer Tanis set out across the North Sea in his own vessel, hunting flatfish. Now though, as I cross the Haringvliet Dam, spotting the trawlers moored in the harbour of Stellendam outside the dyke, something has changed. The sluice I'm driving across remains slightly open even at high tide, letting in some seawater so the fish don't have to wait anymore. They can swim up the river with the current, heading for their spawning grounds.

It's Friday and the fishing fleet has sailed home. But the forest of masts has thinned out, as if someone's taken an axe to them. Kommer's trawler is no longer there, he quit the sea years ago. Fish are now protected by raised lock gates and fishing quotas and he feels cheated. His grandfather fished, his father fished, but now he's stuck at home – though he sometimes crews on other boats when they're a man short. His son still fishes, but on someone else's vessel.

Every Friday morning, Kommer shows up at the harbour to meet the returning fishermen. He sees the catch being landed, crates full of shining flatfish in ice. The fishermen know what he's come for, strange objects snared in their nets: fossils of Ice-Age creatures that once roamed the North Sea steppes when the sea level was eighty metres lower and the Rhine curled northwards over the dry plain to the desolate, frigid coast between the Scottish Borders and the ice of Scandinavia.

Fluctuating sea levels don't scare Kommer. He's a religious man, with a sense of humankind's insignificance in the grand scheme of things. But he's also a fisherman, a hunter. Now that the North Sea hunting grounds are closed to him, he hunts for fossils, not just aboard Stellendam fishing vessels, but also among collectors who scour sand and gravel quarries along the Rhine. Especially in the Upper Rhine basin, the rivers and tributaries between Bingen and Basel.

I've come to meet him because he has a hippopotamus.

*

In front of Kommer Tanis's house there's a little roadside stall like those you see at farm gates, where you can help yourself and leave money. But in Kommer's case it doesn't offer onions, potatoes, tulips or eggs, but the bones of Ice-Age creatures: steppe bison, woolly rhinoceroses, giant deer, horses.

There's a message on a laminated sheet of paper: *To see more, go round the back of the house. Feel free to use the ship's bell.* And on a second sheet next to it: *Dear customer, repeated thefts have made it impossible for me to put my best fossils out here.* There's a photo of a mammoth's tooth, under which he addresses the thieves directly: *Dear thieves, the psychological harm you're causing me is worse than the financial. Because of the thefts, I'm finding it harder and harder to trust people. This makes me SAD!*

Kommer is sitting at the window, reading a copy of *Fishery News*. He gestures to me to come round the back, greets me in the kitchen and starts making coffee. As he chats, putting me at my ease, I wander into the living room, scanning its contents: sofa, coffee table, fireplace, a wall of books, mainly about creation versus evolution, Ice-Age animals and the sea.

No sign of a hippo.

An ancient beam, gleaming softly, hangs above the dining-room table. Presumably salvaged from a wreck, then waxed, it dangles there like a warning; a portent of the shipwreck that hangs above all our heads. There's an object on display on the table beneath the window: the horned skull of an aurochs. A dark hole grins where the snout used to be. I start to spot skulls and bones everywhere: a rhino skull on the floor, the upper jaw of a prehistoric horse in the book-case, teeth pointing upwards. The thighbone of some gigantic creature leans against the wall near the sofa.

He set me down in the midst of the valley, which was full of bones. The words suddenly pop into my head, taking me by surprise. How many years has it been? Was it at the table on a Sunday evening, potatoes and cauliflower steaming in the lamplight? My father, reading from the Book of Ezekiel? Or did my mother consider this Bible text unsuitable for mealtimes? That was sometimes the case. *And the Lord said to me: "Son of man, can these bones live?" And I answered, "O Lord God, only thou knowest."*

Kommer comes in with the coffee. I point at the bones and skulls around me and ask what his wife thinks about them. "She's set a limit," he says, "and this is it. I can add something new, but then something else has to go."

He sits down and sees me looking at the black fossilised bone leaning against the wall. A thick pillar, about mid-riff height, pointing heavenwards. "It's the thighbone of a straight-tusked elephant," he says. "I'm really chuffed about that one."

58

Kommer, now nearing fifty, joined his father's trawler when he was nineteen. So he's been collecting fossil bones and artefacts for nearly thirty years.

"My father always thought I was strange," he says. "'Just chuck it away' he'd say when I spotted a fossil in the net and set it aside. He never understood why I was so thrilled about those finds. Couldn't see my point of view for the life of him . . . That's just the kind of guy he was." He takes a sip of coffee, stoops and sets down the cup on a little table next to the *Fishery News*. "'Such a strange boy' was how he always described me. But I wasn't *that* strange. I might have been the only one in the fleet doing that, but Kees Bok, a fisherman from Ouddorp, used to collect them too, back in the day. 'Such a strange boy', does that ring a bell?"

I nod understandingly. It's instantly clear that we've both been raised in the Protestant faith, though in his case much more strictly. *Such a Strange Boy* is the title of a book I was given to read at Sunday school. It was written by W.G. van der Hulst, a teacher and author of children's books with a Christian message. They were short, moral tales about children who were basically good but who, like all flawed human beings, occasionally strayed from the straight and narrow. Typically they would face a dilemma and then, after a powerful inner struggle or divine intervention, were ultimately moved to "do right". *Such a Strange Boy* was about Hans, a miller's son, whose main weakness was his tendency to daydream. On Christmas Eve he gets lost rowing on a lake in the dark. He misses out on a party and winds up sick in bed, but it all ends happily. (Parties were considered a somewhat dodgy pastime anyway, from a strict Protestant point of view.) Van der Hulst wrote the book in 1917, a year in which, just across the border, hundreds of thousands of daydreamers were being shot to pieces, but the author, anxious to edify the young, clearly had other things on his mind.

Now we've established that I, too, am a child of Calvin, so to speak, I feel I can raise a sensitive issue. I point to a glass case in which a mastodon tooth is softly illuminated. "How do you square all this with the story of Creation, Kommer? Doesn't this create a dilemma? Going by the animal record, the river flowed for millions of years before God created heaven and earth."

"I'm not the kind of Christian who believes that the Creation took place 6,742 years ago on a Monday morning," he says. "When the Bible says it took six days, I reckon that's more about the order in which it all happened. I don't think you can pinpoint the date of Creation by adding up the gene-alogies. That's just impossible. Take those mammoths – we both know they lived in a cold, dry period. And then there's nothing for a while, and suddenly the Pharaohs pop up? There's no getting round it, there must have been many more years in between. I don't know how many, just that it would add up to more than 6,742. Don't get me wrong: I believe that God created all the animals. But he created them according to their kind. That's what it says in the Hebrew, I've been told. It doesn't say: they were all created like they are now."

He looks at me intently. "Only the other day I was think-ing about how there were no carnivores before the Fall. It says so in the Bible. So there were lions that didn't eat meat. Do you really think that God, because He *knew* that humans would fall, anticipated this by creating lions with carnivores' teeth? It seems far-fetched to me that He'd think 'humans are fallible, lions'll be eating meat soon, so I'll just give them carnivores' teeth in advance.' Of course He knew that humans would fall – that's not the point – but that way of reasoning just doesn't seem in keeping with God's nature. So I reckon it's true that carnivores could evolve from herbivores. In the grand scheme of things, those differences in teeth aren't a big deal."

He nods at the bookcase. "I've got lots of books here about evolution and Creation, and I've read them all from cover to cover. There's still a whole lot of things that can't be explained. I always say: when we get to heaven, we'll be told all the answers, then the scales will fall from our eyes. And the reality will be beyond anything we could ever have imagined."

"But the fact that your mastodon could be three million years old . . ."

"That, I don't believe," Kommer says. "Not three million years."

"I hear you've also got a hippopotamus," I say.

"Yes," Kommer says, after a short silence, "the hippopotamus." He slaps his thigh and gets up. He leads the way through the hall and opens a door to a garage that's been transformed into an exhibition space. It's full of drawers, showcases and shelves with collections of skulls, jawbones, teeth, foot and claw bones; not just tastefully lit, but also systematically arranged. To me, a convincing display of the workings of evolution; to Kommer, perhaps a tribute to the diversity and beauty of Creation. We are both impressed.

There was a noise and a rattling; and the bones came together, bone to its bone. And as I looked, there were sinews on them, and flesh had come upon them, and skin had covered them; but there was no breath in them.

"Look," Kommer says, "these are all backs of skulls, so that if I have a bit from the back of a skull, I can see what it is. People come here to identify their fossils based on my collection." He walks to the next showcase. "The more you've got, the more you can compare – and the more you want to have, that's the problem . . ." He points. "From here on it's all predators: a bear, hyena, a wolf. The only thing I haven't got is a lion, so I'm trying really hard to get hold of one."

He halts in front of a large, rather battered-looking skull on the floor. The left bit of the snout has been blown away, as if by a grenade. On the right, the only remaining giant front tooth, nearly as long as a forearm, curves slightly downwards. The eye sockets are as big as two hefty handles.

"And here's the hippopotamus," he says. "Did you know that's Greek for 'river horse'? So a 'Rhine horse' in this case. I wanted that so badly. So when I found it, I was going to give it pride of place on the dining-room table. With a mirror underneath. My wife went with me to collect it, but when she saw it she put her foot down: 'No way am I having that horrible thing on the dining-room table!' I said, 'But Karin, don't you know what this is?' She said, 'I don't care what it is. I just don't like the look of it.' I said, 'But look at those teeth, they're just . . . so amazing!' Then she said, 'We're not having it on the table. I'm sorry, but we're not having it on the table.'"

Kommer laughs and looks down wistfully at the hippo. "Have you seen those molars?" he says.

There are two rows of five teeth, all in perfect condition. You can just picture these animals floating in the river, grazing on the bank.

"You might think it odd, but a hippo's teeth . . ." Kommer pauses. "I get carried away when I see them, always find myself lost for words . . ."

HOME

Streams make the land arable.
When plants grow and animals
Come to drink in the summer,
There humans follow.

From The Ister, *Friedrich Hölderlin*

On the website of the Stuttgart State Museum of Natural History, preparator Thomas Rathgeber's bio states that he was born on the banks of the Nagold, in the town of Calw. Apparently being born on the bank of a river is a fact too important to omit.

The Nagold is a modest little river that, to the chagrin of those who live on its banks, is classified as a tributary of the Enz. What a cheek: the Enz is actually narrower than the Nagold at the spot where they meet! But because of this unfair labelling, the Enz is officially the longer of the two. Had the Enz flowed into the Nagold rather than the other way round, the Nagold would have been both wider and longer than the Enz. Alas, it was not to be. So now the Enz is 110 kilometres long, whereas the Nagold has to be content with a measly 90 kilometres.

This contretemps, which plays out mainly under the leafy canopy of the Black Forest, ultimately dies down in Besigheim, where the Enz entrusts its water to the Neckar, which carries them both off past Heidelberg to the Rhine.

Thomas Rathgeber has left Calw and the Nagold behind. He now works at the museum as a preparator, which means he tends to the prehistoric bones excavated from sand and gravel quarries along the Rhine. I follow his soft, searching voice as he leads the way, in suede shoes and grey pullover, to the bunker where the bones are systematically stored in long rows of filing cabinets. A scattering of stepladders and kick stools allows curators, preparators and visiting researchers to reach the highest drawers which, after a practised tug, slide open with a slight woosh. The rows of cabinets tower nearly to the ceiling and, by turning big wheels, can be moved apart on rails, creating a passageway with rows of identical-looking drawers. A handwritten card identifies each drawer (*Oberrhein, Hippopotamus, Cervidae, Caminus sup, Postcran, Praemolares*). Their bubblewrap-lined insides house the bones of animals that lived in or along the rivers millions of years ago. All neatly ranked by species, jawbones nestling with jawbones, foot bones with foot bones, teeth with teeth. Every bone has a little tag attached to it, loosely tied, with cold, taxonomic jargon in archivists' handwriting: *Dicerorhinus, Mandibula sin. mit dP2 – 4 dP1 – Alveole u. M1 – Keim. Kitsch, Hohwiesen, 6617.6.5.65.14.*

Rathgeber pads along, leading me through the ossuary of the victims of time, evolution and climate change. "Here are the bovine animals," he says in a hushed tone. In passing he brushes a hand along the cabinets, then drums his fingers on one a bit further along:

"And this is where the elephants start . . ."

He stops briefly, opens a drawer. We gaze silently at a drawer full of elephants' teeth.

"Teeth," Rathgeber adds, unnecessarily. "Of elephants."

I nod, but don't ask any questions. My host senses that I'm eager to head upstairs to the museum where, amidst the remains of a world where animals held sway, there's a novelty. Upstairs there's a find from a warm period, about three hundred thousand years ago, before the last ice age. The cold-resistant animals have gone for now. Water buffaloes, hippos, tapirs, Barbary apes, elephants and giant beavers once again forage among the trees and along the rivers. Walnut, magnolia, snowbell and tupelo trees grow on the banks. For the rest, Europe is densely forested. It is in this world that an extremely rare creature makes its appearance on the bank of the Neckar.

A human.

Rathgeber leads me to the exhibition space, pointing out displays of bones in passing, pausing occasionally to scan an information panel, peering over the top of his spectacles. But all at once we find ourselves standing in front of a glass case on a pedestal. There she is, the Steinheim Woman: a skull that is largely intact, except for a massive hole where her left eye would have been. As if a contemporary had crushed her skull with a well-aimed blow from a club. Rathgeber stands there, watching me as I gaze, a smile on his lips. He's proud.

"Is this her?"

"Yes," he says. "This is her."

"A genuine Heidelbergensis," I say.

He stares at me, his smile disappears. He sighs, shakes his head. I've clearly put my foot in it.

*

One summer evening in 1933, in a gravel quarry in Steinheim an der Murr, a small tributary of the Neckar, a skull appeared. The quarry owner's son stopped the diggers and rang Stuttgart's *Naturalienkabinett*, the forerunner of its Natural History Museum. Its head curator, Fritz Berckhemer, knew the quarry well: many elephant, horse, rhino and deer fossils had turned up there over the years. Berckhemer had urged the diggers to keep an eye out for other fossils, and especially for any of early humans. In 1907, the lower jawbone of a hominin had been found in the Grafenrain sand quarry in Mauer, near Heidelberg. Alert workers had spotted it in a layer of sediment, at a dried-up bend of the Neckar. Ever since, the owners of sand and gravel quarries had been on the alert. When Stuttgart got the call that a human skull had been found, Berckhemer grabbed his hat and coat. He arrived in Steinheim that same day, followed the next day by Max Böck, the preparator. They salvaged the skull, scoured the site for other human fossils – in vain – and carried the treasure off to Stuttgart. The diggers could go back to work.

It was the second major find of early human remains along the Neckar. Twenty-six years had passed since the lower jaw had left the Grafenrain quarry, carried off and identified by Otto Schoetensack, an industrialist who in his mid-thirties had resigned as director of the Hofmann & Schoetensack oHG chemical factory in Mannheim and taken up geology and palaeontology. In 1907, he was a private tutor at the University of Heidelberg. Over the course of twenty years he paid frequent visits to the quarry, doggedly but vainly searching among the many fossils for signs of an early human presence. Nowhere did he find gnawed horse bones, charcoal or other indications of human activity. Nevertheless, he urged the quarry contractor, Josef Rösch, to keep looking.

There's a photograph of the Grafenrain quarrymen. Six bearded diggers in baggy trousers and shirts with rolled-up sleeves, a beardless youth and two children, one barefoot. Rösch stands out, the only one with a starched collar, waist-coat and watch chain, smart trousers (a bit the worse for sand) and a short grey beard. He looks well nourished, the others are lean, hollowed out by heavy labour. They stand and sit around their boss, staring at the camera. The spades they're holding look like spears. They've taken their hats off, the sun is shining down on them.

At the bottom right is a thin man with a lived-in face: 52-year-old Daniel Hartmann, "Sand Daniel" to his friends and the other villagers of Mauer. A cheerful chap, hailing from the neighbouring town of Leimen, he would continue to toil in the Grafenrain quarry until the ripe old age of seventy-seven. It was he who dug out a lower jawbone from a pile of sand and gravel and threw it onto the sieve. The jawbone broke in two. Hartmann put down his spade, picked up the jawbone and called his mates over. Rösch strode out of his office to join the group. The circle of men stared at the broken jawbone, which, despite having spent hundreds of thousands of years buried in sediment, had more teeth than Sand Daniel, its twentieth-century finder.

That evening, in Hochschwender, the local pub, he was the centre of attention. "Today I found Adam," he announced – words that the villagers of Mauer could still quote a century later.[*]

The next day, Rösch sat at his desk to write an official letter to Schoetensack, notifying him of the find. It's clear, reading it now, not only that Rösch was aware of the significance of the moment, but also that he felt himself the equal of Schoetensack, who might now be some fancy professor but had started out as an entrepreneur, just like him.

For twenty years now you have endeavoured to find traces of prehistoric man in my sand quarry, seeking proof that humans lived in our part of the world at the same time as mammoths, that is to say Elephas

---

[*] "*Heit haw ich de Adam g'funne.*" (Hartmann was speaking in a regional dialect.)

71

*antiquus. Yesterday such proof was provided, through
the discovery of the lower jawbone of an early human,
extremely well preserved, with all its teeth, more than
twenty metres below the floor of my quarry.*

Schoetensack had waited twenty years for this moment. Now
he was in a hurry. "I caught the next train to Mauer," he
would write a year later in his scientific paper *The lower
jawbone of* Homo heidelbergensis. His excitement at the
find still resonates in the wording of this monograph, in
which he introduces the jaw – and thus the human to whom
it belonged – to the world as *Homo heidelbergensis*.

When naming the hominim, Schoetensack must have
thought that heidelbergensis sounded classier than *sand-
danielensis* (after the finder), *mauerensis* (after the site) or
neckarensis (after the river). The international community
of palaeontologists would have known the name Heidelberg
because of the university, so that must have played a part.
And on top of that, Schoetensack lived there, so in a small
way the early human was named after him. Such a name
reflected glory on the name-giver and the university where
he taught, if only in the capacity of a private tutor. In photographs, the impressively bearded Schoetensack looks every
inch a buttoned-up Victorian. The contrast with the naked
hunter-gatherer who roamed the banks of the European
rivers six hundred thousand years previously could not be
greater. Three years later, his health having gone into sharp
decline, Schoetensack died on the Italian Riviera. He was
never made a professor, though his paper about the jawbone
shot him to international prominence.

In 1948, Daniel Hartmann, who had spotted the jawbone
in the sand, was made an honorary citizen of Mauer on the

strength of that lucky find. A street was named after him, a sculpture was made of his moustachioed head, and on his hundredth birthday, which he didn't quite live to see, the *Rhein-Neckar Zeitung* reported that, through a lucky chance, this alert fellow had done science a greater service than a hundred learned doctors put together.

Heidelbergensis, who in 1908 appeared to be a German river dweller, has meanwhile been found all over Europe and Africa. He wandered the earth for nearly half a million years, roughly between 700,000 and 300,000 years ago. By the time the Steinheim Woman came along, a few hundred thousand years after the Mauer hominim, early human brain growth had accelerated to the point that *Heidelbergensis* had a brain over 1,200 cc in size, enabling him to plan, maintain larger networks, survive ice ages and make finely honed hand axes. On the threshold of the era in which he would exploit the fruits of the tree of knowledge, he had also started wearing clothes.

We call the people who ultimately remained in Europe "Neanderthals" (after a valley of a small tributary of the Rhine, where the first specimen was found). It's tempting to think that they're simply the descendants of *Heidelbergensis,* but DNA research into the remains of contemporaries of the Steinheim Woman found in the Sima de los Heusos cave in Spain reveal that the relationship between *Heidelbergensis* and Neanderthals isn't so straightforward. It may be that both even co-existed in Europe for a time.

So it's not entirely clear how the Steinheim Woman fits into that family.

Hence Thomas Rathgeber's sigh. He's looking over the top of his spectacles again, staring at the skull. He starts to talk vehemently, arguing that it's by no means certain that the Steinheim Woman is either a *Heidelbergensis* or an early Neanderthal. He points to the shape of her skull, which to his way of thinking deviates from both. The inner ear might look more like that of a Neanderthal than a *Heidelbergensis* – or our own – but its shape is unique . . . different . . . how can he put it . . . Steinheimesque.

That's why, as far as he's concerned, the name *Homo steinheimensis* is more appropriate than *Homo heidelbergensis*, not just as a designation of the spot at which she was found, but also of the separate human species that hunted and lived here on the riverbanks, three hundred thousand years ago. And of the Steinheim Woman herself, who, according to a study of her skull carried out at the University of Tübingen, lived and died with a brain tumour the size of a walnut under her crown.

Rathgeber's sudden severity is not nastily meant. It's as if this woman (is the skull even that of a woman?) is dear to his heart. As if he knows her better than anyone. Perhaps it has something to do with the fact that he lives in Steinheim. The woman comes from his village.

A little later I drive through it. Streets of half-timbered houses converge at a central roundabout where, at around five in the afternoon, the rush-hour traffic slows to a halt. In the midst of it all towers a colossal, rust-coloured steel mammoth, erected in 2010 to commemorate the excavation, a century earlier, of an almost intact mammoth skeleton from the Steinheim gravel quarry. A specimen that – in typically Steinheimesque fashion – was soon determined to be a subspecies of the woolly mammoth.

*

Did the Steinheim Woman have a name? From an anatomical point of view – the structure of the vocal tract, tongue bone and larynx – her ancestors would have been capable of speech. That capability would be hundreds of thousands of years old. It is tempting to think that her mother could do more than just say the odd word when it suited her. That she could also make sentences.

I look at the skull of the Steinheim Woman, who would have been in her thirties, and like to imagine that her mother spoke or sang to her when she was a baby. That when she had drunk her fill of milk she looked up with unfocused eyes, trying to make sense of the play of light and dark around her mother's hairline, as babies still do to this day. And that she felt the resonance of her mother's voice in that big, comforting body against which she lay. That she could hear the river murmuring in the background, and bird calls and animal noises from the forest. And that the world smelled of fire.

She had come into the world in a cave, under an overhanging rock or in the shadow of a tree. Her mother, surrounded by other women, sat or lay on the hide of a horse or deer, or on a woven grass mat. A fire was burning to ward off danger. Men hung around curiously, but kept their distance.

There was a word for baby, there was an exclamation for "ow".

Europe was warm when she was born and the rivers were full of clear water. Herds of horses, elephants, rhinoceroses, gazelles and water buffaloes roamed the valleys. Hyenas, wolves and lions lay in wait for straying foals, calves and children.

People were both hunters and prey. They hunted with

long, straight spears, they used clubs to swat birds out of the air – or bash other people. Trapped prey was dispatched with a hand axe, then skinned, impaled on a wooden spit and roasted over a fire.

The Steinheim Woman spent her life beside the river. For years she played and learned, until she was old enough to be useful to the tribe. She was never alone, never by herself on the bank, always within earshot, preferably within reach of the adults. The river courses were the roads, the river valleys the inhabited world. Other tribes lived upstream and downstream. They knew the ones who lived close by well. The rivers went on until they forked, or emptied into other rivers. There, too, lived others, whom they knew less well.

There was prey in abundance, entire flocks grazed along the banks, at dusk monstrous great beasts emerged from the forest's edge to drink. The hunters eyed them hungrily. The bigger the kill, the longer they could live off it before having to risk life and limb again, before having to face another fight. Hunting was dangerous: no animal wants to die, animals are seldom alone, bulls are as terrifying as storms, an elephant can crush you in a second, and a fresh carcass will immediately attract lions, hyenas and wild dogs from every direction.

Fires were the only answer. Fires were the walls of home for the Steinheim Woman. She learned to find the tinder fungus which, when ground to powder, easily catches sparks from a flint; she learned the strength and vulnerability of stones, the lines along which they split, the spot you have to hit if you want the stone to submit to your will.

No-one knew for sure what would happen tomorrow, but the moon waxed and waned, the sun rose and set, the stars revolved silently, hot and cold seasons always returned, along with storms and droughts.

76

As did the rain, sometimes for weeks on end. The river swelled, the current knocked down trees, swept away banks, rolled boulders from their places. The waters rose, became a flood, the land shrank and grew swampy, hampering horses, water buffaloes, aurochs and deer in their movements, sometimes even forcing them into the forest. The people huddled together, trying to keep their smoking fires alight. In that small world everything smelled of rain and woodsmoke. The rain, the river, the wind in the trees, everything whispered and rustled, the only other sounds were the cries of animals. No-one noticed the solitary jaguar that lurked motionless between the dancing leaves and watched the fires die down.

In times of drought the river grew calmer. Hippos wallowed in the deepest pools or trotted along the banks on their short legs: big, angry, dangerous creatures. The meadowland had grown wide, the river narrow. Migratory fish lay in the shallows, waiting for rain. A herd of deer roamed in search of grass. Four hunters with burning branches put them to flight, driving them under a cliff from which others hurled boulders. The deer they hit were finished off with spears and hand axes.

One day – by now the Steinheim Woman had reached adulthood – they saw strangers approaching from upstream, walking along the bank. Every now and then people living alongside other branches of the river would come downstream to the plains. There they met with others, some for the first time. They had strange words for hand axes, horses, daughters, sons.

Stones were swapped, weapons compared. There were elephant hunts. But there were also fights. Not everybody survived these encounters.

As soon as the days started getting shorter, everyone went home: back along their own rivers, upstream, downstream; to their own caves, hunting grounds and valleys. Like ripples from a stone flung into a pond, they fanned out along tributaries radiating from the single big river in the centre where they had sought and found one another. They walked all the way to the southern coast of the North Sea, they walked to the high mountains in the south, they walked to the capillaries of the tributaries in the east. To where the rivers stopped. Beyond that point, towards where the sun rose, an unknown world began where people used incomprehensible words and didn't know how to make a hand axe.

The young woman of Steinheim had got a headache on the journey, a headache that wouldn't go away, not even with a paste made from the bark of young willow branches. The pain flowed like water from somewhere under her crown. She bore a baby – having been got with child during her sojourn at the big river – but she was not vigilant enough and it was taken by a lion.

It got so bad that she couldn't use one of her arms properly, and she could only whimper in pain. One night she left the camp, walked out of the safe circle of fire and, in the moonlight, climbed to the bank overlooking the river. The water was high, its murmur filled the night. She climbed higher and higher, below her the water churned, scraped along a wall of gravel and sand.

In the camp, amidst the fires, those who remained heard her scream, then the crash of a bank collapsing, boulders rolling. Then only the murmur of the river and, in the tree-tops, the sound of approaching rain.

THE SKATING BEAR

Now spread thine azure folds and glass-green robe, O Rhine,
and measure out a space for thy new stream:
a brother's waters come to swell thee

From Mosella, *Ausonius*

When I walked the dog as a teenager, I would duck into Teesinkbos opposite our house: a 24-hectare estate with an abandoned, decaying mansion at its heart. The grounds were in a pleasant state of neglect: a comfortably sized wood that had grown wild, with ancient oaks and beech trees, ferns and blackberries, pockets of heath with scattered birch trees, lingonberries and wood anemones, a stray deer in a clearing, squirrels leaping from tree to tree, enormous rhododendron bushes, the occasional kingfisher by the lake and, of course, the Teesinkbeek – the brook that ran through the estate.

"You're always hanging around there. What do you get up to?" a classmate of mine asked in the playground. The girl who was eavesdropping – I was too shy to look her in the eye – burst out laughing and turned away. The classmate also lived opposite the wood, but he never went into it.

I would walk there with my dog, always following the brook. No attempt had been made to tame it; the stream meandered through the wood at will. There were ridged patterns in its sandy bed, and along its many bends the water had carved out steep banks the height of a man, in which sand martins made nest holes. The November storm of 1972 had uprooted a lot of trees, a couple of which had fallen across the brook. In the years that had since passed they'd sprouted multicoloured toadstools.

Walking upstream along the right bank, I'd occasionally

teeter across one of the fallen trees to the opposite side, where I felt as if I was on alien territory. Stranded on the familiar bank, the dog would bark at me.

Rarely could I persuade anyone to come along with me. When at last I got a friend to join me, I tried to impress him by swinging over the brook like Tarzan, on a low hanging branch. But I grabbed at thin air. The retreat in soaking-wet trousers was so humiliating that my friend said goodbye to me at the edge of the wood and took a different route home.

Even my dog didn't always enjoy these outings. Especially if I sat down for a while on a fallen tree at the water's edge, scanning the meadow, hoping to spot a long-eared owl on the branch where it had perched the year before. She would look at me, stop wagging her tail, let her ears droop and sigh.

Now that Kim Cohen had ticked me off about my excursion to the source of the river, I realised my strolls along the Teesinkbeek had actually been trips along the Rhine. Because the Teesinkbeek transports water from the outlying swamps – via the Boekelerbeek, the Oelerbeek, the Twickelervaart, the Regge and the Vecht – to the northern branch of the Rhine delta: the River IJssel.

The river is more than just its bed, Cohen had impressed on me, it's the entire catchment area. The Rhine is also the tributaries that flow into it from the Alps to the North Sea, the mountain rivulets of Austria and Liechtenstein, the muddy woodland brook in the Black Forest, sprinkler water from the vineyards of the Alsace, snowmelt from the Fichtel Mountains on the Czech border, rainwater dripping from the roofs of Nancy into the sewers, droplets from the sacred well in the crypt of Echternach Abbey, waste water from a

Düsseldorf car wash, drizzle falling on the Meuse, which joins the Rhine just before reaching the sea.

And the Teesinkbeek.

The only true source of the river is the rain that falls on us, from France to the Czech Republic, from Friesland to Italy.

There are maps of the Rhine and Meuse river basins. You can find a good one on Wikipedia. It's the map of a land no-one knows – a land whose borders have been dictated by the interplay of water, gradients and gravity. With a bit of imagination, its shape resembles a skating bear which, balancing on one leg with outstretched forepaws, is gliding westwards.

The basin is at its narrowest around the bear's left knee, a corridor of a mere hundred kilometres between the realms of the Danube and Doubs-Rhône; further north, it fans out eastwards and westwards. Level with Frankfurt, the bear sticks his right leg in the air, his toe grazing the Czech border. His outstretched forepaws reach from the capillaries of the Sambre in northern France to the upper reaches of the Lippe near Paderborn. His skate rests on Italy's northern border. The tip of his ear pokes up into Friesland, while his muzzle dips into the North Sea.

By some happy fluke, the basin's north–south and east–west axes intersect at the Lorelei. So the rock is not just the cultural, but also the cartographic centre of the river.

*

At the westernmost point of the river basin there's a sleepy northern French village with red-brick, tile-roofed houses. There's no-one around, in most homes the windows are still shuttered. The town square (actually as triangular as a wedge of cake) is dominated by the towering façade of the church, which looks in need of renovation. Sporting a pointy little gable, the *mairie* vainly tries to rise above the adjacent houses. Next to it there's a big, squat, warehouse-like building. The sign on its façade says SALLE DES FÊTES.

A westward turn-off from the main road just outside the door of Café des Arcades ascends, after a mere hundred metres or so, to a bridge that crosses a stream and a canal. The stream's cloudy water flows slowly northwards, the water of the canal dimples silently in front of a lock. To the left and right, willows grow along the banks.

The village is called Ors, the stream the Sambre. It springs from the woods to the south-east and, before curving north-east to end in the Meuse at Namur, it bends westwards through the meadows.

At the lock, the Western Front Association has erected a brick memorial whose plaque reads:

On 4th November 1918, the British 32nd Division
crossed the Sambre-Oise canal here, at Ors,
in the face of strong opposition. During the
assault four VCs were won. Among the
casualties was the poet, Lieutenant Wilfred
Owen MC, 2nd Battalion Manchester Regiment,
who was killed on the towpath on this side
of the canal about one kilometre to the
north of the bridge.

A glance at the map shows that a kilometre to the north, the Sambre, and the canal dug next to it – to connect the waters of the Rhine and Seine – lie slightly more to the west than in Ors itself, though not even by fifty metres. The towpath runs along the dyke that was raised between the Sambre and the canal.

If Wilfred Owen was killed on the towpath, that means he crossed the Sambre but never reached the opposite bank of the canal.

I walk along the towpath for a kilometre, to the spot where Owen fell. On the left, the Sambre flows beside me at walking pace; on the right, the canal's calm surface is disturbed only by the occasional fish snapping at a fly.

A kilometre further and not much has changed. A little footbridge leads across the river; in the meadow there's a small, walled cemetery for fallen soldiers. I listen. It's just as silent as in the village. A winter sun shines on the white gravestones.

"Move him into the sun," suddenly comes to mind, "Gently its touch awoke him once." They're the only lines of Owen's that I know by heart. I walk along the rows of graves but don't see his name. Google tells me he's not buried here, but in a corner of the village cemetery, among the dead of Ors.

The precise details of Owen's death are unclear. Did it happen on the towpath? Was he on a raft when the Germans opened fire on his battalion? Was he dragging planks for an emergency bridge? Did he fall on land, or slide into the water? The film *Regeneration*, based on the books by Pat Barker about Siegfried Sassoon and Wilfred Owen in World War I, shows him half in the water, his dead eyes gazing skywards in a cloud of flies.

Whatever the case, it happened at about eight in the morning, a week before the Armistice. Army command knew that the war was over, but the troops were made to fight on until the last hour.

*

It was already November 1918 by the time the 2nd Manchesters arrived in the war-torn woods around the village of Ors, fifteen kilometres east of Cambrai. A month earlier, the Allies had breached the Hindenburg Line, the last line of German defences on the Western Front, and during that hellish operation these men had crossed the Saint-Quentin Canal. The unit was led by Second Lieutenant Wilfred Owen, then twenty-five years old. When he wasn't fighting – and that was the case on most days – he would write poems and letters to his mother. But on 29 September all hell broke loose, and it was only on 4 October, after the battle at the canal, that he could reassure his mother:

> My darling Mother, as you must have known both by my silence and from the newspapers which mention this Division – and perhaps by other means or senses – I have been in action for some days. [. . .] It passed the limits of my Abhorrence. I lost all my earthly faculties, and fought like an angel.

In August 1918, despite being under no pressure to do so, Wilfred Owen had reported for active service. He had already served at the front in 1916, had been wounded and traumatised, and for a while had been treated for shellshock at Craiglockhart Hospital in Edinburgh. After his treatment, his doctor, William Rivers, considered him fit for light duties, but Owen didn't want light duties. He wanted to go back to the front. The poet Siegfried Sassoon, with whom he had become friends in Craiglockhart, threatened to stab him in the leg to prevent him from leaving. But Wilfred went. "With great & painful firmness I have not said you goodbye from England," he wrote once he was safely in France. "If you had said in the heart or brain you might have stabbed me, but you said only in the leg; so I was afraid."

Owen reported to the Manchester regiment, witnessed the Allied breakthrough on the Western Front, and was still alive. "My nerves are in perfect order," he reassured his mother. "We are marching steadily back. Moreover the war is nearing an end."

This was true. After the breach of the Hindenburg Line, the German command, too, knew that it was over. It was now a question of getting out diaries and agreeing a date and time when it would be convenient for everyone to stop shooting at each other.

That wasn't yet the case when Owen, his nerves in perfect order and in line for a medal, arrived at Ors, though it did preoccupy him ("We have the *Times* of Thursday, and the strange news makes us feel that the Rumble on the horizon may cease any hour. I'm listening now, but it still goes on, a gigantic carpet-beating").

It had rained heavily, and Owen and his men had had to spend nights in the open. Since breaching the German lines, the landscape they'd passed through resembled a black-and-white photograph being gradually coloured in. Meadows were turning green, farmsteads were getting new roofs, working horses stood ready in farmyards, children played. The streams, babbling alongside him to the left and right, were full to the brim, as if during these last days not only his men, but also the rainwater were travelling eastwards.

The trees here were still alive, clad in autumn foliage.

Everywhere there was light and colour, like a memory, a trick of the senses.

But as they neared the retreating German front, the war once again stole all colour and life. Heavy bombardments had thinned out the woods and blasted craters in the farm-land. When they were half a day's march from Ors, the battalion halted. Owen had reached the westernmost border of the basin of the Meuse, and thus also of the Rhine. The Sambre ran somewhere through this shattered landscape. A canal had been dug parallel to the little river, connecting it with the Oise. In Ors there was a lock and a bridge.

Yet another canal. Yet another opposite bank with wait-ing enemies. The battalion kept away from the water, hid in a forester's cottage, explored no-man's-land by night. Communication with headquarters was difficult, but the postal system still functioned.

Owen wrote his last letter in the cellar of their hideaway. He'd spent the previous nights outdoors, with only a few planks to keep the off the worst of the rain, but now he was warm and dry, surrounded by his men, the air thick with smoke from the fire on which the cook was trying to boil potatoes. He told his mother that he and his personal servant had eaten the chocolate she'd sent him, that he was saving the Malted Milk for the days ahead. It was cosy and cheerful in the cellar, men were laughing and joking, an old soldier with a walrus moustache was peeling potatoes and dropping them into a pan. Keyes, the cook, was chopping wood for the fire. "It is a great life. I am more oblivious than alas! yourself dear Mother, of the ghastly glimmering of the guns outside & the hollow crashing of the shells. There is no danger down here, or if any, it will be well over before you read these lines."

On the morning of 4 November, at around six o'clock –

the sun had not yet risen – he and his battalion made for the Sambre and the canal. The last kilometres of his life led through battle-scarred, gently rolling terrain with a scattering of willows and rivulets. The horizon gradually lit up in the east. A new day. Owen and his battalion reached the Sambre a kilometre north of the village. There was no sign of life on the opposite bank, only a farm where nothing stirred. There had been hellish shelling a month earlier, when the Allies had crossed the Saint-Quentin Canal, and the locals were still keeping their heads down. It wasn't strange, therefore, that the farm looked so quiet. Using rafts and ropes, the soldiers began to build a bridge.

Halfway through their labours, the farm windows opened and German soldiers concealed behind them opened fire on the battalion. And that was how Wilfred Owen died, on the border of the realm of the Rhine, a week before the gigantic carpet-beater of the war finally fell still. His mother received his last letter on 11 November, the day the Great War ended.

*

Ors cemetery is packed with family graves, their headstones bristling with laments for the dear departed. The villagers make clear, to themselves and to each other, that they will not forget the dead. This is a farming community, so there are numerous marble sheaves of corn, doves with twigs in their beaks, and even a lone gold tractor. Plastic flowers in porcelain vases, extinguished candles in glass holders, rain-sodden ribbons. It's strange: so much space in this agricultural landscape, with its woods and meadows, yet so little room for the dead. They are squeezed together, the graves are crooked, the gravel paths cramped.

But in one corner, where the war dead are buried, it is green and peaceful. The white gravestones stand in a straight row, as if along a canal.

On Owen's grave there's an open question: shall life renew these bodies?

Outside the cemetery there is an information panel featuring a photograph of the forester's cottage, which – at the request of the mayor – a British artist has painted entirely white. Two walls flank a footpath that curves downwards, so that visitors descending to the cellar see white walls rise to the left and right, like in a trench. Some lines from his final letter have been engraved on them. In the cellar, which looks just as it did when Owen spent a happy night there, the young poet's words to his mother resonate.

I hope you are as warm as I am; as serene in your
room as I am here; and that you think of me never in
bed as resignedly as I think of you always in bed.
Of this I am certain you could not be visited by a
band of friends half so fine as surround me here.
Ever
Wilfred x

The photo of the white house on the information panel in the cemetery has been vandalised, scratched with a stone or a knife. There is no-one around. The church tower is dilapidated, there's a smell of fire, somewhere a cock crows.

This is the westernmost point of the Rhine.

Almost eight hundred kilometres east of Ors, in the Fichtel Mountains near the Czech border, is Bischofsgrün, the river basin's easternmost settlement. The White Main headstream bubbles up from the Fürstenbrunnen, a wellspring on a slope of the Ochsenkopf, just outside the village. From there it trickles eastwards, taking in water from the brooklets of Mount Seehügel, then changes its mind and does an about-turn, heading first north, then westwards. At Steinenhausen, after meandering along for about fifty kilometres, the White Main joins the Red Main and the two rivers flow together for more than five hundred kilometres, past Würzburg and Frankfurt to Mainz, to empty into the Rhine.

Every year, on *Rosenmontag* – Shrove Monday, the highlight of Germany's pre-Lent carnival festivities – Bischofsgrün prides itself on building Europe's largest snowman, a ten-metre high colossus with a giant blue 220-kilogram hat on his smiling, red-cheeked head. The snowman is called Jakob. Here, *Rosenmontag* has become "Snowman Day".

It's not exactly an ancient custom – it started in 1986 – but in that short space of time it's become deeply rooted. Even though warmer winters mean there's now not enough snow in Bischofsgrün itself for the construction of a monstrous snowman, the villagers cling to the tradition. Every year, the mayor Stephan Unglaub gives permission for twenty lorry-loads of snow to be scooped from the northern slope of the

Ochsenkopf and delivered to the main square where Jakob will stand. He's put together by ten self-appointed "snow farmers" using a long-armed power shovel. Then the partying starts, and the slow decline sets in.

With each passing day, Jakob looks a little worse for wear, like a corpse gradually caving in on a malfunctioning cooling bed. He sweats, his smile becomes fixed, he sags, he melts. After a couple of days his giant hat is removed with the aid of a cherry-picker, to prevent it from sliding off his melting head and crushing a passing villager. Meltwater trickles through the cobbles of the square, dribbles into man-holes and is ferried through drains to the brooks outside the village. Eventually the White Main carries what is left of Jakob to the Rhine.

*

1 July, 1785. Three hikers on the Ochsenkopf are looking down at the village of Bischofsgrün. It is late afternoon and they're tired. A thunderstorm threatens. On the way to the summit they slaked their thirst at the Fürstenbrunnen, the wellspring of the White Main. The cool water refreshed them, and they carried on with a burst of energy.

But now they're standing here with light heads and hot legs, looking down.

"Bischofsgrün at eventide," the eldest of the group remarks. He is Karl von Knebel, an ex-soldier who, disappointed in his military career, took up a post at the ducal court of Saxe-Weimar as steward and tutor. He taught Frederick, the younger of the two princes, until he left home at just seventeen, an embittered loner who rode out of the courtyard without looking back.

Von Knebel remained in the court's employ. Frederick's elder brother, Carl August, was embroiled in a power struggle with his mother. His father having died very young, he was now the Duke of Saxe-Weimar, and the eighteen-year-old was trying to free himself from maternal interference. He had his own ideas about rulership and a penchant for wine, women and song. This resulted in a lot of parties, court intrigues and awkward conversations with mother, a state of affairs that placed heavy demands on Von Knebel's diplomatic skills.

The hike up the Ochsenkopf marks a short break in a journey on foot to the spa town of Karlsbad, where the young duke and his mother will take the waters, as they do every year. Though now twenty-eight, the duke is as hot-tempered and unruly as ever, and still chafes under his mother's disapproval.

Now that he's away from the court, though, he relaxes. Von Knebel has presented the walking tour in the form of a geological study trip. The duchy of Saxe-Weimar is seriously strapped for cash – not least thanks to Carl August's lifestyle – and the duke's hopes are now pinned on the copper and silver mines of Ilmenau where, after decades of neglect, a new shaft was dug and operations resumed. However, after a year of toil, the mine has yet to yield a grain of ore. So Von Knebel and his fellow travellers are visiting more successful mines en route to Karlsbad.

He stands on the Ochsenkopf and looks north, out over the roofs of the village, towards the towering Schneeberg, the only mountain in the Fichtel range that's higher than the Ochsenkopf. There's a distant clap of thunder. Von Knebel exchanges looks with his friend Johann von Goethe, whom he had introduced to the young duke in 1775, and then persuaded to leave Frankfurt to take up a position at the court of Weimar. Von Knebel hoped that the presence of the illustrious author would have an edifying, restraining effect on the duke's lifestyle. But if anything Carl August, who was entranced by Goethe at first sight, became even more wildly impulsive. And Goethe, whose party trick was to intoxicate listeners with the dizzying flow of his words, driving them into raptures or frenzies, was initially happy to bask in the duke's admiration.

It wasn't the duke but the writer himself who concluded, after a few years in Weimar, that a life dominated by mood swings and ungovernable passions just wasn't sustainable. Two years after his arrival, inwardly devastated by the death of his sister Cornelia – his rock – he fled the court for a trip to the Harz mountains, where he scaled the Brocken on a clear winter's day, and during his climb found solace in the immutable solidity of its granite. So different to the people around him, so different to his internal chaos. The words thudded in his head to the beat of his climbing footsteps: the deepest . . . the oldest . . . the slowest . . .

The Brocken, which towers above the rest of the Harz range like an Olympus, provided Goethe not only with a sweeping panorama of the frozen north-German landscape, but also with a deep insight into his own soul. On reaching the summit, he allowed himself to be transported by the notion that the granite mountain he had conquered rested on the Earth's core, and that he, seated on the summit, was in touch with the great interplay of the unfathomably slow, soft-spoken forces of nature.

He would have liked to have sat there until his internal tempests had entirely subsided, but after a while hunger and thirst got the upper hand, and with renewed interest he looked down at the valley with its wells, streams, fields and inns. And of course at the people who lived there, who were not pondering how deeply anchored the granite peaks were in the bowels of the earth, but instead were just getting on with life.

He descended, satisfied his bodily needs at an inn, mounted his horse and galloped back to Weimar. Carl August forgave his *Geheimrat** his unannounced flight from court, subsequently even putting him in charge of reforming the army, road building and mining.

He had little time to write. After years of silence, his first publication was his opening speech for the new mine in Ilmenau. "This shaft that we are opening today will become the portal through which one descends to the hidden treasures of the earth – the portal through which those gifts of nature, hidden so deep in the ground, will be brought to light," he told the miners. "We are now able, if God so wills, to descend and ascend this shaft, and to gaze with rapture on that which, until now, we could only imagine."

Standing next to Von Knebel, he looks down on the village below, on the homes of the people of Bischofsgrün. The third man in the company, a young botanist called Friedrich Gottlieb Dietrich, has sat down. He opens his botanising chest and inspects his finds: wild garlic, enchanter's nightshade, barberry and box. Von Knebel, an amateur geologist, has chipped off rock specimens along the way: gneiss, quartz and slate. And collected a little pouch of yellowish, crumbly sandstone from which tin is mined on the western flank of the Seehügel.

That morning the men had set off from Wunsiedel, where

* Privy Councillor.

they'd taken rooms at Hotel Einhorn on Maximilianstraße. The path they had followed up to the Ochsenkopf led from the realm of the Elbe to that of the Rhine. Then, as now, the watershed lay on the summit of the Seehügel, more than a thousand metres above sea level.

During the descent the men arrived at the Seehaus, the workplace of the tin miners. There they saw how the miners washed the metal out of the stone by diverting a mountain rivulet into a trench they had dug and filled with pulverised tin ore. The debris was carried away by the water, and the heavier tin sank.

Before coming to Weimar, Goethe had eulogised mountain streams in the poem "Mohammed's Song", which described how, like twinkling stars, they sprang from a joyful world above the clouds. He painted a lyrical picture of brooks chasing colourful pebbles in their descent, joining with fellow rivulets and cascading gaily over marble rocks to gush into the valley, where they hastened past flowers and fruitful meadows to the silvery plains and the eternal ocean.

This mountain stream in which the tin ore had been washed no longer bubbled gaily, but oozed downwards in a blubbery trickle, clouding the infant White Main for many a league past Bischofsgrün.

As he stood there, aching feet planted on the sedimentary stone of the Seehügel and eyes fixed on the dirty water sloshing past, *Geheimrat* Goethe, newly responsible for the mines of Weimar, seemed far removed from his romantic younger self. On leaving, he was presented with a little lump of tin, which he fingered in his trouser pocket as he gazed down at the village roofs.

More thunder rumbles overhead, this time close by. As the first drops rattle on their hats, they begin their descent. With the wind at their backs they hasten past the Fürstenbrunnen, leaping over the White Main when they reach the bottom, then climb up again along the stream of cloudy mine water, on their way to the watershed at the top of the Seehügel. On the other side, the water dripping from their jackets will seek its way to the Elbe, but right now they're still at the easternmost point of the Rhine, and the rain which – as the poet saw it – dances and gaily descends on their shoulders, hurries downwards on its long journey to the "eternal ocean, which with open arms awaits us".

Seven hundred and fifty kilometres north-west of the Seehügel lies the south-western corner of Friesland, the most northerly point in the Rhine basin. The water of the IJssel travels at an almost imperceptible pace along the old sea dyke to the Lorentz locks, where it flows onto the mud flats at low tide. That unfolding ribbon of freshwater, rich in nutrients, doesn't just come from the Alps, the German hills and the Vosges. It also contains rain that fell behind the dykes and has been pumped into Lake IJssel via sewers, reservoirs and canals.

Just like the rest of the Dutch coast, this most northerly landscape of the river basin has been shaped by the sea in a test of strength with the delta. During the ice ages the sea sometimes disappeared for more than a hundred thousand years, but when the Earth warmed, the North Sea basin filled up again and the estuaries returned to our regions.

This has happened dozens of times since the Rhine established its current basin three million years ago. High tide halted the river and the river pushed back. The ribbon of Rhine water fanned out across the incoming tide. Fine sediment – mineral specks that had been scraped off up-stream and had whirled along in the river, sometimes for more a thousand kilometres – was caught in that stalemate between saline and fresh. It hung motionless, clumped together and was washed ashore in spring tides and storms.

In this way, the coastal region gradually heaped up plains of rich clay.

This delta country, drained and tamed, has become flat, low and monotonous. There's more sky than earth. The heavens cover the landscape like a translucent dome, edges resting on the distant horizon. Clouds sail slowly past, masquerading as animals, preachers, capsized galleons. Sometimes they descend and graze the fields, dark-grey veils advancing inexorably, heralding rain.

Humans are small in this place. They are taciturn, but filled with longing. For thousands of years they have grown grass for hay here, have herded, milked and slaughtered their cows. Before the dykes enclosed the delta, the land would be flooded at spring tide. You can still see the artificial dwelling mounds that people built as places of refuge.

This is the realm where Tsjêbbe Hettinga learned to talk, until he started to write poems. And where he learned to see, until he lost his sight. In the landscape he conjured in his poems, milk churns still stood by the side of the road, lapwings tumbled above the hay meadows and Friesian horses grazed around the farm. His father filled the evenings with stories, told in Frisian. A language that belongs to an estuary, with words from upstream and from across the sea. "My father was a storyteller, his mouth a river," Tsjêbbe's brother Eeltsje wrote to me.

Eeltsje, too, became a poet.

The Hettinga family farm is in Burgwerd, a village clustered around a low mound on the Bolsward canal, with a cobbled high street, a pale-brick church opposite a stately mansion, a disused farm in the village centre, a garage, a firm that makes machine parts, rows of farmworkers' cottages, street lanterns along the water's edge, a bridge, well-tended front gardens, recycling bins and cyclists who raise a hand in greeting as they pass.

It was early April, the air was as clear as in a dream. It seemed to me that, between the houses, I could see the curvature of the Earth in the distance. Apart from a few trees sticking up around farms, and the spires of neighbouring village churches, I had an unbroken view of the line where the land sank away below the horizon: "a high bright-blue sky dazzling the eye like a glass dome," as Tsjêbbe Hettinga remembered it in one of his poems, "the endless acres of grass, with here and there a farm obliterated by the green-beaded brushes of trees." Tsjêbbe's father bred horses, glossy black Friesians. They gallop through Hettinga's poetry, slam holes in the tarmac. Horse and landscape become intertwined, providing each other with metaphors.

> There he stands: his withers higher than the breast
> of dunes, his flanks
> And muscles tauter than the thin blue strap on the
> northern
> Horizon, his back a wild expanse, his liniment-soaked
> neck
> A saga [. . .]

And in the background of nearly every poem is the sea – always lighting up, galloping, on its way somewhere.

The lines quoted above are from his epos "The Father Horse" which, depending on how you read it, is an ode to his father or to a long-lost springtime, or to the stallion Bernlef, born and bred on the farm. Five times the Hettingas sold the stallion, five times they were overcome by regret, and five times they bought him back at a loss.

The last time Bernlef returned to Burgwerd was when Tsjêbbe's father had just died and his body was laid out at home. In the stillness between his death and funeral, the timeless clatter of hooves rang out in the farmyard. As if Bernlef had come back to fetch Father. There they went, father and horse, to the St Francis Basilica in Bolsward, and from there down the cobbled street along Dijlakker canal, past St Martin's Church, past the statue of the Frisian Renaissance poet Gysbert Japicx, to the cemetery on the edge of the little town. Bernlef black as coal, mane flapping, head leaning into the sea wind, neck gracefully curved, a rugged power held in check beneath the reins.

The landscape has changed since the days of the eighth-century heathen bard Bernlef, when the south-western corner of Friesland was still called Wininghe, but the impact of the struggle between river and sea has not been erased. Unless you count the sea dyke – a straight line in the west – that has held the river and storm surges at bay since the eleventh century. Otherwise, the delta remains as it was, an endless expanse in which the same horses trot with the same proud, rough-hewn elegance, and the same mounds raise farms up above the meadows.

What Bernlef wrote, back in the Dark Ages, has been lost to memory. But there was surely a link with what Tsjêbbe Hettinga was to write twelve hundred years later in his poem "Tusken twa Seeën" (Between two seas), set in a dream-like landscape in which river (the Ee) and sea still battle each other as if a dyke had never been built:

These days no-one knew whose hands had bound
    the reeds
One sea-light evening – the swallows flying high – and
    Woven them into a basket. A basket
With moon-round prows that at night became a cradle
    Launched on a still silent stream between two seas,
Where it was tugged to and fro by the shifting tides.
    With the last breath of wind that rustled within,
The boat-rocking reed bestowed its ear-tickling words
    On a fisherman's son, a boy secretly
Given to the sea, who lapped up the stories of
    The fish as they leapt past fiery rainbows and
Over the breasts of dwelling mounds, farms and churches,
    While cloud-hallowed water conferred its blessings.
Swooping seabirds taught him to speak: above the land's
    Shrieking cries of "Wininghe" and the gleeful "Ee"
Of the broad babbling river that gave him his voice.

RUBICON

When it reaches the Ocean, the Rhine separates into several channels, thus forming a large number of sizeable islands. Most are inhabited by fierce barbarian peoples, some of which are thought to live on fish and birds' eggs.

From The Gallic War, *Julius Caesar*

Around the first century AD, the aurochs that plodded to the banks of the delta on hot summer days to drink or cool off were nearly as big as the female mammoths with whom they'd shared the steppes for tens of thousands of years. By the time the last ice age had made way for the Holocene – an era of tepid rain, a retreating ice cap and a North Sea coast that moved ever southwards – the mammoths had died out. But the aurochs had hung on. Around them, the world was changing. The rising sea had pushed the Rhine estuary back landwards. Forests shot up, first willows, then birches, eventually oaks. The aurochs learned to eat leaves, acorns, even bark.

The meandering Rhine fanned out into a jumble of routes – some silted up, some new – depositing sediment in its course. The wind raised river dunes and, in warm springs, the meltwater of the hinterland washed away chunks of land and young trees, but on either side the landscape remained open and covered with juicy, nutritious grass. There the aurochs bulls, enormous beasts over six feet in height, reigned supreme. Their horns, as long as a human arm, curled forwards over their ears, ready to impale anything that came within sight. Such as other bulls, competitors with whom they would test their strength when their cows were in heat.

The rivers had posed no lasting obstacle to their distant forebears, as the ice-age summers were short and chilly, and the ice on the slopes upstream melted only very gradually. The river was often shallow enough for the animals to wade through.

That changed as the ice age came to an end. Rain clouds massed on the horizon above the rising North Sea, sweeping showers across the steppe. Much of the ice in the Alps, the Black Forest and the Vosges melted. The rivers became fuller, branched out, looked for new routes, deepened. The babbling, light-green streams of the ice age turned into murky barriers of angry, rushing waters. The bulls on either side hesitated on the banks, could no longer find a spot shallow enough to wade through. They stared at one another, their bellows echoed across the water.

*

Aside from Caesar's flying visit in AD 58, the first Roman commander to push through to the Germanic bank of the Rhine and stay there was Drusus, stepson of the emperor Augustus and brother of the future emperor Tiberius. He arrived in the Low Countries with his troops in 12 BC. The Rhine carried him smoothly to the delta, but when he got to the north it proved tricky to transport his army any further by water. They ran into shallows and silted-up streams, their ships got stuck in the mud. When asked about deeper navigation channels, the people who'd been watching from the banks could only shrug helplessly, used as they were to travelling by punt. They were Frisians, a Germanic tribe living in what we now call North Holland, Friesland and Groningen. Their world consisted of dunes, swamps and dwelling mounds at the edge of the northern ocean, where their territory bordered that of the hot-tempered Chauci.

Drusus got on reasonably well with the Frisians, judging by the fact that they occasionally helped him free his heavy vessels when they ran aground on mud flats on northern punitive expeditions against pirates or the Chauci. But Drusus was enough of a Roman not to let nature get the better of him. He built jetties, army camps and eventually forts. And he made a pact with the Frisians: he would leave them in peace as long as they supplied a small number of men for the Roman army and paid an annual tax of ox hides.

Apart from cattle and grain, these northerners had little that the Romans wanted. Why settle for flatfish that had been pegged on sticks and dried in the wind; porridge made of grass seeds, buckwheat and linseed; green cheese flavoured with sheep dung; and cloudy beer made with rainwater if you could have a constant supply of olives, wine, fish sauce, lentils, figs and grapes brought over the Rhine from the south? Friesian cows were the only thing they had any use for: as beef to eat and as hides to stretch across their shields.

The Frisians, who bought peace with ox hides, were an easy-going Germanic coastal tribe. They not only complied with the Romans' demands, but went so far as to embrace their fashions, even their gods. In the Frisian Museum in Leeuwarden, boxes full of finds from dwelling mounds show just how eagerly they embraced novelties from south of the rivers. Not just decorative objects like ornate cloak pins, but also beautiful, slim, muscled, nude figurines of the war god Mars, which were given a prominent – or secret – place in the shadowy living and sleeping quarters of Frisian homes.

Thus the Romans and Frisians lived side by side. The Frisians supplied cattle, the Romans built forts. Apart from that, very little happened. This honeymoon lasted for forty years, almost two generations. It's not so hard to imagine what the Roman troops' lives were like in the sparse forts along the river. Some of the legionaries had probably been there for years: in winter, stamping their feet and rubbing their hands in watchtowers or sweating in peat-fuelled bathhouses, on summer days – drizzly but pleasant – cheerily embarking on the annual tax-collecting tour of the surrounding farms. Soldiers who had learned where the sand ridges ran through the peat bog, who knew which points they could ride to and which you could only reach by poling a punt. Around them, the landscape of dunes, marshes and grassland stretched out on all sides, larks climbed and twittered above their helmets, and the sky was everywhere. Over time they'd got to know the farmers and their wives by name, would engage in macho banter with their sons, pay their daughters compliments, swap cloak pins for a roll in the hay. After years of communicating through gestures they at last knew what to say, what not to say, and to bow their heads at the spot where the ancestors were buried.

That kind of life, of soldiers getting comfortable at an outpost, came to an abrupt end in AD 28, when they were assigned a new commander. Olennius was a centurion from an elite family, hailing from the south – an impatient youth in search of fame and full of loathing for this godforsaken place in the north. See him gallop past the forts with his mounted escort, red cape fluttering in the north wind, cursing the drizzle, cursing the state of the roads, cursing the delay at yet another small ferry crossing.

The troops in the forts, he notes, are sloppily shaved and have a lackadaisical look about them, one or two legionaries have incipient paunches straining against their breastplates.

When he asks them how relations with the barbarians are, he gets evasive, wishy-washy answers. And the Frisians who hang around the forts are impertinent giants who tower above him and don't lower their eyes in his presence. They smell strongly of barn, sweat and curdled milk. Asked who their gods are, they nod in the direction of the river, of the forest.

And then, one evening in one of the pathetic, rickety little forts on the river, a spine-chilling, deep roar echoes across the water in the chilly twilight. Olennius climbs a watchtower and spies a monster on the opposite bank; a bull standing there in the evening mist, so huge that Olennius's steed could trot between its legs without bending its head. Smoke comes from its muzzle. With its black hide gleaming and steaming in the golden light of sunset it resembles one of the fire-breathing bulls of Colchis, the bronze monsters that Jason had to tame.

That night, pitch-black as the road to the underworld, he's kept awake by the grunting of the bull. Olennius hates his fear, fights down vexing memories: his mother and her bedtime stories, the Frisian who disrespected him yesterday. He gets up, once again climbs the watchtower and stares across the river. The moon has risen, the river is silver, something stirs on the opposite bank, a beaver slaps the water with its tail.

The next morning he summons his officers and issues his orders. From now on there's to be no more fraternising with the natives. He, centurion Olennius, will no longer be satisfied with the measly, second-rate ox hides that the locals have for years been fobbing off on the tax collectors. Olennius's command to the Frisians was more literary than practical: "Bring me the hide of an aurochs!"

The listening men stand to attention, thinking: this is going to end badly.

The Frisians weren't familiar with the tales of Hercules, Jason and Theseus, and how they were sent off by fearful kings on quests to kill monstrous, bloodthirsty bulls in the hope that they would die in the attempt. But Olennius had undoubtedly been raised with these stories.

How did he see himself when he arrived at the fringe of the Roman Empire? As a civilised ruler in a distant outpost, a mouthpiece, perhaps, of his all-powerful gods? Didn't he know the fate of the men who'd ordered Hercules, Jason and Theseus to kill the wild bulls? Had he forgotten that the heroes didn't die, that they came back in one piece and that the king who'd sent them on the quest had ended up in pieces in a cauldron?

Perhaps Olennius thought that he could get away with it in this northern garrison on the edge of the world, because these barbarians weren't classical heroes, so wouldn't be protected by Juno, Neptune, Diana or Apollo.

"Bring me the hide of an aurochs!" he said to every Frisian he encountered. And thus – as these things go in classical tragedies – he sealed his own fate.

*

The Romans were newcomers with strange food, ornate jewellery and attractive statuettes of deities. Their ships, armour and forts must have struck fear into the northerners. But there were greater and older fears with which the Romans couldn't compete: a holy respect for the monsters that lived along the rivers and the forest edges.

Tacitus, who narrates this history in his *Annals*, doesn't

give us the name of a Frisian war chief who takes it upon himself to oppose Olennius. Doesn't identify a valiant warrior sent off on a quest to kill aurochs in the lands above the northern bank of the Rhine, who then returns, not with ox hides, but with an army.

That's a pity, but it's also telling. If there had been a single leader, Tacitus would undoubtedly have named him. Instead, he speaks about the Frisians in general: "That same year, a people beyond the Rhine, the Frisians, broke the peace."

In Tacitus' account there was no leader egging the Frisians on, but a panic that engulfed the whole community, eventually exploding into revolt. The order to kill the bulls apparently touched on a taboo so strongly and widely held that the Frisians preferred to hand over their diminutive cattle, possessions and even children rather than attack the aurochs.

"At first they were surrendering just their oxen," writes Tacitus, "then their lands; and finally it was their wives or children delivered into slavery. This led to rage and protests; and when this proved fruitless – to war. The soldiers who were there to take the tribute were kidnapped and nailed to gibbets. Fearing the wrath of the Frisians, Olennius fled, taking refuge in a fortress called Flevum."

The settlements in the delta were still a backwater, a place where very little happened, when Olennius first arrived. The nearest sizeable military camp upstream was Oppidum Batavorum, where the city of Nijmegen would later arise.

In the year AD 28, there were only three fortlets along the river between Oppidum and the sea, *castella* where you could moor vessels, billet soldiers and crush or parry revolts from behind wooden palisades. The fortified harbours that would, in time, be built upstream from the various Rhine estuaries were intended to intercept pirates coming upriver from the sea to raid settlements.

Flevum was one of the earliest military camps, on the Proto-IJ, the most north-westerly branch of the Rhine, which discharged into the sea near what is now the Dutch town of Castricum. Until the 1970s no-one knew for sure whether there really was a Fort Flevum in Holland, or whether it existed only in the realm of Tacitus' imagination.

But that changed with the discovery of the fort in 1974, and a final excavation during the construction of the Wijkertunnel. Archaeologists stumbled on the remains of a fortified harbour on the spot where the Proto-IJ had flowed. The dig revealed evidence of violence: there had been a battle for the fort, somewhere between AD 25 and 30. Exactly as Tacitus had related.

The archaeologist who dug up the fort and wrote his doctoral thesis on it is called Arjen Bosman. Besides being an archaeologist, he's also an ex-Unifil soldier. He served in Lebanon, so he knows first-hand what it is to stand on a watchtower far from home, looking out over a landscape that appears deceptively tranquil. He, too, left the protective walls of the fort to make contact with nearby villagers, often communicating through gestures to overcome language barriers. His mission was to win the locals' trust and preserve the peace simply by being there.

It might have been a long time ago, but he's still got a soldier's mindset, he tells me, as he leads me to the place where Fort Flevum once stood. Below us, fenced off, is the southern entrance to the Wijkertunnel. Where once Rhine water flowed through the Proto-IJ to the sea, the North Sea

Canal now lies motionless, a breeze rippling its surface. The only reminders of that ancient landscape are the reeds that have shot up along a ditch, the bridleway running alongside the road, and the groves of willow, their slender leaves whispering in the wind. Bosman, blending archaeological expertise with military experience, looks around him and tries to conjure up the past.

"Here you see a branch of the Rhine." He sweeps his hand in the air as if, through words and a gesture, you could reshape the earth. "The landscape is quite flat, the higher dunes aren't yet there, just a few older dunes along the coast. The grass is boggy, especially here, near the river."

He turns his gaze to the north-west. "There on the bank is Flevum," he says. "A few pontoons and jetties stick out into the water. The pontoons are connected. You can enter the fort by walking along the jetties. And there . . ." – he points over my shoulder – "on that side there's a rampart and a canal and towers, so the soldiers in the fort can keep a close eye on the surrounding area. In the event of a threat – pirates coming up the river, say – they can come out to engage with the enemy, either in their vessels or overland."

We stand there for a while, silently taking in the scene. I try very hard to picture what it would have looked like back in Roman times, but it's not easy. At this spot, "a sizeable force of Romans and allies stood watch over the ocean coastline," Tacitus tells us. What you see now, though, is the big white office block of the Verkeerscentrale Noordwest Nederland, a road and waterway traffic control centre. There are no longer any soldiers on turrets, only technocrats behind tinted glass staring at monitors. The North Sea Canal is a tamed, impassive presence. A roll-on-roll-off ship from Japan, packed with cars, approaches from the direction of the IJmuiden sea locks. A monstrous box, it towers high above the tugs towing it towards Amsterdam. A moped, dwarfed by the giant backdrop, buzzes along the road. Its driver, a helmetless, beer-bellied man with a hand-rolled cigarette in the corner of his mouth, has two fishing rods with him. He's probably heading for IJmuiden pier.

Bosman, unflappable, continues his historical sketch: "This branch of the river flows into the North Sea at Castricum. Weakly though, because the estuary there is beginning to silt up. The population has grown enormously since the Iron Age. So it's pretty busy by the time the Romans arrive. In the regions on either side of the river, the water has become fresh enough for the Frisians to raise cattle and grow grain. And that makes it easier for the Romans to settle here – there are enough people who can supply them with cattle. You can tell from the bone fragments we found that animals were herded into the fort and slaughtered there. All of them scrawny little cows bought from local farmers."

The idea that the excavated fort is the same Fort Flevum that Tacitus wrote about is almost too good to be true. "We haven't found a single inscription mentioning the name," Bosman admits. "It would of course be fantastic if we'd stumbled on a ruined entry gate, or a barrier arm with a sign saying 'You are now entering Fort Flevum, please report to the sentry.' Sadly, that's not the case. But I'm sure it *is* Flevum."

I look at Bosman. His mention of a barrier arm suggests that the Unifil soldier is beginning to take over from the archaeologist. "We found more than five hundred lead shots, in a pattern that suggests a battle took place. On top of the layers of waste that had been dumped there, we found human remains in the port basin, soldiers who'd been killed and left behind. And we found bodies that had been dumped in the fort's wells. A combination of those finds indicates a highly unusual situation: battle, a traumatic incident."

A bus approaches the stop, halts and disgorges a passenger who looks around, disorientated. It sets off again.

"In one of the wells we found the remains of two men," Bosman says, more softly. "And one of those men must have had a coin with him, because it was lying next to him, in mint condition, which is to say virtually new, minted between AD 22 and 30. So this could have been in the year AD 28."

"We're standing on the wall," I say, "and here come the Frisians. What do we see?"

"A horde of barbarians," says Bosman, "and we think: we're outnumbered . . . what the hell do we do? We've been trained to fight, but now we have to fight from inside our fort, which we're not used to. We've been trained to advance on the enemy with our mates, in a column, behind a wall of shields . . . but *they're* now advancing on *us*, and there probably aren't enough of us, so we'll have to use slingshots to fight them off, and we haven't got enough shot either, so we'll have to quickly make some more – we can use sticks to poke holes in the sand, or if we haven't got a stick, our fingers – and we'll fill those holes with molten lead, because luckily we *do* have enough lead, since we repair our own boats here, and pretty well, too . . . they're attacking from the south-west now, targeting our gate, we manage to beat them off, but they're still coming . . . they keep coming, across the water, those guys have got little boats too or perhaps they're swimming across, but luckily we've managed to hit a few of them, because we saw them fall overboard . . . we'll just let them bob around there in the water, because we're much more bothered about our mates who are getting killed too, right next to us, because yes, they're fucking throwing spears at us, and shooting arrows at us. We're not used to that here, but they won't get in, luckily we can keep them out, we can even do that from the water. And, thank the gods, we've just heard that reinforcements are on their way."

And then the storytelling stops. Bosman blinks, and is silent.

*

TACITUS WRITES:
When word of this reached Lucius Apronius, governor of Lower Germany, he called in detachments of legions from the upper province, along with an elite group of auxiliary infantry and cavalry. He then shipped both armies together down the Rhine and marched with them against the Frisians. The siege of the fortress had by now been raised, and the rebels had left in order to defend their own territory. Apronius built embankments and bridges in the neighbouring estuaries, creating a route solid enough to take the weight of a more heavily armed column. He also ordered the Canninefate cavalry, along with all the German infantry serving in our ranks, to wade through a ford and attack the enemy from the rear. But the Frisians were already in battle formation, and were driving back the allied squadrons and legionary cavalry sent as reinforcements. Then three cohorts of light infantry were sent into the fray, followed by two others, and, after an interval, by the mounted auxiliaries. This was

a strong enough force – had they attacked together. By arriving in stages, however, they failed to strengthen the resolve of the disordered units and were themselves being swept away by the panic of those in retreat.

The Roman commander did not seek retribution, nor did he bury the dead, even though many tribunes and prefects, and some outstanding centurions, had fallen. It was subsequently learned from deserters that nine hundred Romans had been cut to pieces in a grove they call Braduhenna, having drawn out the battle to the following day. Also that another contingent of four hundred soldiers who had occupied a villa belonging to Cruptorix, a former mercenary, fearing that they had been betrayed, had died on each other's swords. After that the Frisians enjoyed some cachet amongst the Germans.

The first documented revolt in the Low Countries – which started because of cattle, money and honour – was a resounding success. Emperor Tiberius never even took revenge, according to Tacitus. On the contrary, the dispute was soon patched up. The Romans might have abandoned Fort Flevum, dismantled the harbour and poisoned the well with bodies, but a few years later a new fort arose close by. In the Frisian Museum in Leeuwarden there's an ancient artefact from the northern Netherlands – a Roman writing tablet found in Tolsum, Friesland – inscribed with a contract written in Latin, concerning the sale of a slave. In short, for a while, the Romans and the inhabitants of the northern Netherlands acted as if nothing had happened. Until Rome realised it perhaps made sense to see the Rhine not just as a transport route to and from the north, but also as a border. That the delta comprised a land above and a land below the rivers: an austere coastal region of cattle, dwelling mounds, dried flatfish and rainwater, and a gentler region south of the river, of figs, wine and heated bathhouses.

Crossing the Rhine is a solemn occasion;
one trembles in anticipation of those terrible words:
You have left France.

From Germany (*1813*), *Madame de Staël*

The Rhine is north-western Europe's own Rubicon. It divides territories; crossing it is seldom without significance. It separates Switzerland from Austria, Liechtenstein from Germany, Germany from France and, in the Low Countries, the Protestant north from the Catholic south. Even to Caesar, who'd never before been to Gaul, it was clear that the world on the western bank of the river was different to that on the eastern.

"Gaul is divided into three parts," he writes in *The Gallic War*, "one of which the Belgae inhabit, the Aquitani another, and the third a people who in their own language are called 'Celts', but in ours 'Gauls'. The River Garonne divides the Gauls from the Aquitani, and the Marne and the Seine rivers separate them from the Belgae. Of these three, the Belgae are the bravest. [. . .] Their closest neighbours are the Germans who inhabit the land across the Rhine, with whom they are continually at war."

When, in 58 BC, Ariovistus, leader of an alliance of Germanic tribes, met with Caesar in Gaul, the situation was extremely tense. The fact that Ariovistus and his warriors were on the wrong side of the river could only mean that he was on the warpath. He himself was quick to admit this, claiming he would have preferred to be with his kindred, the Suebi, in the lands between the Elbe and the Rhine, but that there had been good reason to leave home and hearth. According to Ariovistus, he had been invited to cross the Rhine by the Sequani, a Celtic tribe. The Sequani were at war with the Aedui, another tribe of Celts, and hoped to defeat them with the help of Ariovistus' troops. That hope proved justified, but after inflicting a defeat, Ariovistus and his Germans did not return to their own bank of the Rhine. On the contrary, more and more Germans kept coming over.

Caesar ordered Ariovistus to return to his side of the river with all his troops and mercenaries, and when the German warlord refused, during a heated conference held on horseback, a battle ensued. Caesar won, despite being seriously outnumbered, and Ariovistus fled across the Rhine in a small boat. Ducking into the forest, he disappeared from history.

After the battle, Caesar sent ambassadors across the river to demand that the Germans surrender their warriors. They came back empty-handed, with a simple question from the Germans: the Rhine marked the boundary of the Roman Empire. If Caesar didn't want them crossing into his territory, why was he telling them what to do on their own turf?

"Who do they think they are?" Caesar bellowed. "We'll cross over. They won't feel safe anywhere."

A piqued commander crossing a river naturally wants it to look heroic. So preferably at a spot where the banks are solid, the other side clearly visible, and the water clear and shallow. Apart from the stretch between Mainz and Bonn, though, the valley of the untamed Rhine was still an overgrown bog several kilometres wide, in which countless streams crisscrossed each other like a tangle of spaghetti. Standing on the bank, you often couldn't see the other side:

there were too many trees and it was too far away. It was a treacherous swamp in which even the most heroic army would soon be reduced to a pathetic band of lost souls, mired horses and bobbing sandals.

Which is why Caesar, boiling with rage and imperial pride, detoured to the clear banks of the central Rhine valley, probably a little upstream of Andernach. The water was deep and fast-flowing, but the banks and numerous islets in midstream were stony and solid, and the other side was close and clearly visible.

"Caesar had determined to cross the Rhine," Caesar afterwards wrote of himself, "but he felt that crossing by boat was too risky, and moreover that it was beneath his dignity or that of the Roman people. So despite the extreme difficulty of constructing a bridge (because the river was so broad, swift and deep), nonetheless he concluded that he must attempt a crossing by bridge – or not take his army across at all."

Ten days after the first tree trunks arrived, the bridge was finished. It wasn't the first time that a conqueror crossed the Rhine, but it is the first documented bridge. There it stood, a triumph of Roman engineering not previously witnessed by the Germans. It made a deep impression and therefore had the desired effect. The Suebi fled into the woods. Caesar burned their villages, cut down their buckwheat, corn and peas and, after eighteen days, felt he had achieved his objective. He marched back to the western bank and had the bridge dismantled.

*

Caesar would wade through the Rubicon a mere six years later. But he had now set the tone for a military operation that, pulled off anywhere between Basel and the sea, would guarantee a heroic reputation. Commanders who had accomplished this risky feat liked to show off their valour, for example in a painting, because the event lent itself excellently to being immortalised on canvas. The situation is clear and easily grasped. There is an army, there is a river, there are two banks, one here, one over there. The advance party has detached itself from its own bank and is crossing to the other side: a martial snapshot coalescing with the moment at which their commander attains fame. He is usually located on a picturesque elevation with a good view of the crossing. He is of course on horseback, usually somewhat to one side of the picture – not only to allow his men to pass on their way to the river, but also not to obscure the view – because of course the onlooker needs to be able to see the troops below, wading through the river or marching over the captured bridge. The commander is always pointing a baton towards the other side, lest anyone should think the soldiers were crossing of their own accord.

During his campaign against the Dutch Republic, Louis XIV sent his army across the Rhine at Lobith on 12 June, 1672. A painting of the scene by Adam Frans van der Meulen* shows Louis kitted out in gold brocade, left hand nonchalantly on hip, mounted on a rearing white steed. With his right hand he points a field marshal's baton at the opposite bank, while around him cannon blaze and below him his troops – also on horseback – wade and swim through the water towards the territory they seek to con-

---

* His impressive job title was *Peintre des Conquestes de Sa Majesté* – Painter of His Majesty's Conquests.

quer. By a happy coincidence, the painter has caught the king at the precise moment that he looks over his shoulder, seeking eye contact with the viewer. He is the centre of everything, encouraging his men on, vanquishing the Rhine.

Joseph Parrocel, a contemporary and competitor of Van der Meulen, who also portrayed the crossing, opted for more or less the same composition – the sovereign on a high point, with the crossing below – though in his painting the action around Louis is somewhat less hectic. Here, too, the royal horse rears, here, too, Louis points his troops towards the other side. But instead of a gold-brocade coat, he's wearing a shiny suit of armour and elegant black thigh boots, and his horse isn't white, but brown. Although there's less going on in this picture, the scene is more dynamic than Van der Meulen's. The sky above the Republic on the other side is almost Van Gogh-like. In both paintings, the river is so shallow that the horses can mostly wade across, only having to swim for a short stretch. Which is accurate – the summer of 1672 was a dry one.

The noble commander-in-chief above, the troops down below, the rearing horse. The Duke of Lorraine, who crossed the Rhine at Strasbourg in 1744 during the War of the Austrian Succession, was similarly portrayed by Johann Tobias Sonntag: at an elevated spot, on horseback, pointing across the river with his baton, while down below his troops march across bridges linking the riverbanks via islands in the middle. His horse rears, a Moorish servant carries his armour, day dawns in the east.

How different things would be half a century later, when the French revolutionary army crossed the river at the same place. Various engravings were made of this event, in which the sovereign pointing the way to his troops is conspicuously absent. Instead, the focus is on the revolutionary infantry, who are undertaking the crossing in wobbly, overloaded little boats. The frail craft are surrounded by floating bodies, soldiers fire from the foredecks. Of course there's no sovereign. He remains behind in the fatherland, his head separated from his body. It's all about the spirit of the people, driven onwards not by a king, but by inner fire. High above everything, a gale chases heavy clouds from west to east. The men have the wind at their backs.

Engravings made a year and a half earlier show the French revolutionary general Jean-Charles Pichegru and his legionnaires crossing the frozen Waal on foot into the Dutch Republic on 10 January, 1795. Here, too, the focus is largely on the men themselves, though there is a drawing showing Pichegru pointing at the opposite bank with drawn sabre. Huddled in their coats, the soldiers trudge across the river. It is −15° C.

After the Napoleonic Era, classical paintings of army commanders made a brief comeback. Wilhelm Camphausen portrayed Field Marshal Gebhard Leberecht von Blücher and his Silesian army crossing the Rhine at Kaub in pursuit of Napoleon in early January 1814. Blücher and his steed are right in the middle of the painting, on a nicely elevated spot above the river. The soldiers, once again mostly on horseback, are making their way down to Pfalzgrafenstein castle, a picturesque building with snow-covered turrets, in the middle of the icy river. Blücher, too, points the way. Not with a baton, but with his pipe, presumably in between puffs.

His horse isn't rearing, by the way. The painter, himself a former hussar, knew that you couldn't keep your balance on a rearing stallion while gazing nonchalantly over your shoulder, one hand on your hip, the other holding a baton. Or at least that it would look silly.

Blücher is still there, incidentally, on the bank of the Rhine. His statue – erected in Kaub with the posthumous permission of the Prussian King Wilhelm I – remains proudly in place, though over the years, weather and bird droppings have turned it green. Either the sculptor wasn't up to horses or the budget didn't run to an equestrian statue: he stands firmly on his own two legs, pointing commandingly at the Rhine. He's not looking at the river, but at something lower down, to one side, presumably his troops as he orders them to advance. His cloak flutters slightly in a gust of wind. A display case with text and photos, installed by Kaub's Blücher Museum, informs the visitor that, standing on the bank, Blücher declared: "Here and nowhere else will the bulk of my Silesian army cross the Rhine, so that I can continue to pursue Napoleon in his own country!"

By that time, Blücher had already earned the reputation of being outspoken and hot-headed, friendly towards his soldiers as a rule, but restless and impatient in battle. His biographer and contemporary, Karl August Varnhagen von Ense, who wrote fawningly about Blücher's character and looks (. . . tall, slim figure . . . wonderful skull . . . marvellous forehead . . . piercing, ever-darting and yet in the main benevolent light-blue eyes . . . the character of a war hero . . .), could not, in his exhaustive description of the man, skate around the fact that his voice was gruff and harsh, lisping – due to a lack of teeth – and deafening when he was angry. So it was a loud, toothless command that preceded the famous crossing.

*

The last time that Blücher – or at least his likeness – was surrounded by a crowd in Kaub was on 8 June, 1894, when his statue was unveiled. Exactly seventy-nine years had passed since the Battle of Waterloo, at which Blücher had arrived just in time to help Wellington beat Napoleon. Imperial flags fluttered, a band played, a podium had been erected and a steamship lay moored in the river, its gangplank decorated with canopies and bunting. Speeches were given from a dais at Blücher's feet. Emperor Wilhelm II was not present, but his emissaries were. The programme promised a "festive meal on the festive steamer", followed by a "festive ball". For a brief moment, Kaub was the centre of the empire, because here, and nowhere else, Blücher had crossed the Rhine and chased off the French from the opposite bank.

It's quiet around the statue. Flags still wave, but they're neither Blücher's nor the empire's, nor even Germany's, but UNESCO's. Rhine Gorge UNESCO World Heritage Site, they proclaim. More than two centuries after Blücher's crossing, the Upper Central Rhine Valley is not only of consequence to Germany, it seems; it is now world cultural heritage. So a bit French, too.

And because there are no longer any troops marching along the banks of the Rhine, merely the odd poodle or terrier being walked on the immaculately maintained lawns, Blücher looks less like a general shouting "March, march, in God's name!" lispingly but deafeningly at his hesitating soldiers, than an elderly inhabitant of Kaub, vainly pointing out a thrown stick to his reluctant dog.

There he stands, the hero of Waterloo, immortalised in the moment just before his crossing of the Rhine. Here and nowhere else.

Dear SHAEF,
I have just pissed into the Rhine River.
For God's sake, send some gasoline.

Patton to Eisenhower, 24 March, 1945

A border that coincides with a river – this makes sense. A child can understand that over there, on the opposite bank, another world begins. The river is an ally, it keeps the other at a distance. Back in 1814, any customs officers or soldiers on the French side of the Rhine must have felt a pang of anxiety when they saw Blücher's sappers starting to build a pontoon bridge. One moment they felt secure, the next afraid.

That juxtaposition of security and fear – two sides of the same river – is timeless: from the Germans watching in shock as Roman troops crossed at Mainz in 406; to the dread felt by the Dutch as the Rhine began to freeze in 1672, paving the way for Napoleon's advancing army; to the German troops in Erpel, panicking as they saw the Allies on the other side of the river at Remagen in March 1945, making their way down to a bridge that was still intact.

To get a sense of their panic, you need only to look at the eyes of the German Captain Willi Bratge, in the film clip where he recalls seeing American soldiers storming onto the bridge at Remagen on the afternoon of 7 March, 1945. Bratge was stationed on the east bank of the Rhine, in command of thirty-six men charged with guarding the railway bridge over the river. These were soldiers who had been injured in previous skirmishes, and had been sent to the Rhine to convalesce. Some weren't in a fit state even to hold a gun or pull a trigger – let alone run away.

The end of the war was in sight. The Allies were nearing the west bank of the Rhine. Taking a leaf out of Caesar's book, Eisenhower was considering crossing the Rhine at Andernach as well as at Düsseldorf, as the Russian army had done a week and a half after Blücher, on 13 January, 1814.

He dreaded it, everyone dreaded it.

Even in the twentieth century, the Rhine was as terrifying an obstacle for an advancing army as it had ever been. The bridges had been destroyed, the crossing would have to be done by storm, in small boats and on pontoons, or by airborne landings. Everyone knew how that had ended in Arnhem.

Strangely enough, the fact that the Ludendorff bridge at Remagen was still intact came as a surprise to the Allies. Captain Karl Friesenhahn, Bratge's comrade-in-arms, and his 125 sappers had even worked tirelessly to lay planks across the bridge, so that ordinary vehicles could drive over it. They had rolled out the red carpet, as it were, for the Allied troops. Only when they came dangerously close could the bridge be blown up, was the German order.

When, in the space of few hours, the Americans captured the village of Remagen and the bridge still hadn't been blown to smithereens, Lieutenant Karl Timmermann – the American grandson of a German who had emigrated to Nebraska – was given the dubious honour of taking the bridge, contrary to all orders from top brass. The villagers warned him that Friesenhahn planned to blow it up at 4 p.m.

The fact that the bridge had been designed for military purposes in the run-up to World War I is evident from the gun slits in the four bunker-like towers at each end. Recesses for explosives had even been built into the bridge, to facilitate its destruction should a retreat be necessary. On the eastern bank, the bridge led directly to a railway tunnel through a steep granite rock face that rose in a tangle of basalt columns.

That morning a lorryload of explosives arrived for Captain Friesenhahn, but it mistakenly contained only half the amount Friesenhahn had ordered, and moreover the wrong type. The lorry driver had him sign for a consignment of Donarit, rather than the much more powerful TNT.

Willi Bratge tells the story of that day in "The Bridge at Remagen", an undated, black-and-white American documentary which can be found on YouTube. He's sitting in a classroom, in front of a fully chalked blackboard. You can make out the words *Frühling*, *Wiese* and *Blumen*: spring, meadow and flowers. As the camera pans out, an abacus appears to his left. After the war, the defender of the Ludendorff bridge became a primary school teacher.

His short, grey hair is combed back flat, his ears stick out, his cheeks are clean-shaven. His eyes grow wide as he sits there, against a written backdrop of meadows, flowers and spring, talking about that day on the bridge at Remagen. No flowers, no meadows, only panic and fear. He's looking at the camera, but his gaze is directed inwards, at images looming in his memory. He starts to speak louder, to shout, he's there again at the bridge, the *Wacht am Rhein*,* the fate of the fatherland in his hands. The Americans are on the opposite bank, he sees them hesitate. Friesenhahn remotely detonates a bomb near the bridge entrance on the far side. They're briefly driven back. But when the smoke clears, they're still there.

He shouts to Friesenhahn to blow up the bridge, but

* "The Watch on the Rhine", a patriotic anthem written in 1840, urging all Germans to defend the Rhine against enemies.

Friesenhahn says he doesn't have the authority to take that decision, he needs orders from a superior.

That morning, an officer, Major Hans Scheller, had reported to Bratge, announcing that he had come to take over command. But he offers anything but leadership, retreating deep into the tunnel in the granite rock face, where he paces back and forth. Desperate now, Bratge sprints 350 metres through the dark tunnel, which is full of invalid soldiers and civilians. Gasping for breath, he tells Scheller that the bridge must be blown up. Scheller traces circles in the sand with the tips of his boots. Bratge yells that if need be he'll give the order himself, at which Scheller shrugs.

"Do what you must."

Bratge runs back through the tunnel, back past the invalids, men, women and children. He dashes out into the daylight, he screams at Friesenhahn: "Blow it up!"

You can picture teachers and pupils being alarmed by Willi Bratge's panicky voice as the recordings in the quiet primary school progressed. They halt in the corridor, stand on tiptoe, peep into the classroom through the chalk-dusted panes. Bratge's sitting there, shouting at everyone to take cover, to lie on the ground in the tunnel. And then there's the bang, a huge explosion, a pressure wave that blasts through the tunnel like a hot whirlwind.

And it goes quiet.

Joseph DeLisio, an American sergeant who witnessed the explosion on the west bank, relates in the documentary how he saw the bridge lift off its foundations before a huge cloud of dust and debris blocked it from view. When the dust cleared, and the bridge was somehow still standing, the infantry battalion commander, Major Murray Deevers, gave Lieutenant Karl Timmermann the order to storm the bridge with his company.

There are black-and-white photographs of Timmermann. He has the looks of an actor: James Dean, say, but in a turtleneck and helmet. "Do you reckon you could get your company across that bridge?" Major Deevers had asked.

Timmermann hesitated. "What if the bridge blows up in my face?"

Deevers didn't answer, he just turned and walked away. No commander on a horse pointing the way with a baton. No reckless determination. Just hesitation, shame, fear.

Yet Timmermann goes. The route he must take is clear. They open fire on the entrance to the tunnel where the German troops are holed up, and the first men run to the other side. There's a film of them crossing the bridge: at first they hesitate, but then you see them running, rifles over their shoulders, one soldier with a knapsack, another with a bundle of some kind attached to his belt, helmets on, looking ahead to where grenades rain down on the tunnel entrance.

This is the moment you see in Bratge's eyes, the moment when he's trapped in the tunnel with his thirty-six convalescent soldiers, when he realises that all is lost, that the Rhine has left him in the lurch and that the land behind him now lies open. He was the *Wacht am Rhein*, and he has failed. He puts a hand to his throat, thumb on one side, index finger on the other, squeezes slightly and is silent.

He knows he's a goner.

Major Scheller, who has made a run for it, will indeed be executed. Bratge is taken prisoner of war, survives, and will end his days as a schoolteacher. While on active service in Korea, Timmermann was diagnosed with testicular cancer and flown home. He died in 1951, at the age of twenty-nine.

*

There is a wooden cross on the Erpeler Ley, the volcanic basalt cliff through which the railway tunnel leads. It's been put up quite recently. A brass plate states that it's a "cross of peace", erected by the municipality of Erpel, to commemorate the soldiers who died on and near the bridge. A well-tended lawn gives the little viewing plateau a solemn touch. A nearby café is aptly called *Bergesruh*.

It has become an outing for day-trippers who don't mind a short hike up through the woods to look down over the river and the village of Remagen. A fence has been put up to stop rambunctious children from falling over the edge, and to give older folks something to lean on as they look down. People have chained little padlocks to the railings. There are already more than a hundred of them, and they look set to spread like moss. A German and a European flag flap overhead.

Two men stand by the fence, shoulder to shoulder, looking down. Friends, probably. Or perhaps neighbours. They discuss the history of the place, conclude that it would be easy to fire at the other side from this height. After about ten minutes they've exhausted the topic of the war. One starts to talk about work, the other about a garden chore, and then they fall silent, gazing a little while longer.

The cliff, the river, the village, the distance.

CANALS

Tom Hazenberg has driven ahead of me from his archaeological research office on the becalmed Old Rhine, straight through Alphen – past office blocks and shopping centres, and along winding little residential roads bobbled with traffic humps – to the leafy entrance of the Archeon, an open-air archaeological museum. He strides into the museum grounds, holds a door open for me and ushers me into a long workshop that smells of wood and preservatives.

There, in muted daylight, under a sheet of canvas, lies the Roman barge *Zwammerdam II*, a flat-bottomed vessel twenty-three metres long, its wide bow and stern curving slightly upwards, like a ferry boat. The wood is black with age.

This ship, together with two other barges, was discovered half a century ago when archaeologists excavated the harbour of the Roman fort Nigrum Pullum. Other finds included three dugout canoes: fishing boats made of hollowed-out oak trees. The dig took place in Zwammerdam, a village built on the spot where army commander Corbulo built the fort in AD 47.

The find made international news, because the wrecks were remarkably well preserved. Named after the place where they were found, the Zwammerdam ships were sawn into bits and spent decades submerged in preservatives in lightproof containers.

Thanks to this thorough soaking, the timber will probably

survive another few thousand years, and the first of these vessels has now been re-assembled and restored in a public viewing gallery in the Archeon. The bits that had rotted away have been replaced with new pieces of timber, carefully reconstructed by hand. No matter what angle you look at it from, it is truly impressive. Not just big, but also well designed and as timeless as the river itself. Anyone who knows the Rhine sees it mirrored in this ship, which lies ready, as if in dry dock. It's a massive craft, radiating ambition. It looks unstoppable. Built to glide effortlessly over shallows, it can also be powered by sail (to judge by the base of the mast) and there's space at the stern for the rowers and the helmsman to manoeuvre, moor and set off again.

Like any ship that appeals to the imagination, you can sense, even on dry land, how it would move when afloat. I'm seized by the urge to set sail, to surrender myself to this boat and to be carried along by the river. I know that too much time has passed for me to know how a Roman would think and feel, but the movement of this ship on the river, the life vibrating through its construction, the creaking of the timber, the water splashing on the bow – it was no different then than now. The *Zwammerdam* no longer ferries across water, but across time.

"You can almost feel it going up and down," I say to Hazenberg.

He nods. "I was there when the boats were dug up – I was just a kid at the time."

The boy who watched the excavation in the 1970s is now a man with his own archaeological research office. In 1996 he headed a dig in Leiden at the spot where the archaeological park Matilo marks the footprint of the Roman fort beneath it. Just like Nigrum Pullum, Matilo was a military settlement on the south bank of the northern branch of the Rhine, strategically located at the mouth of the Corbulo canal. Hazenberg found the timbers of the embankment, the spot where vessels were moored, the possible location of a bridge over the canal, part of the road to the coast.

"Tacitus wrote that Corbulo had his men dig that canal to keep them busy," Hazenberg says. "And that he was frustrated at not being allowed to cross the Rhine anymore. But I don't think the master plan behind the canal and the forts along the river had anything to do with the Frisians – it was all about Britain. That was where a wealth of minerals lay, the prize that the Romans had set their sights on. What did the north have to offer, other than cows?"

He gazes at the *Zwammerdam*. "Taking to the sea was a challenge to start with, and there's no way that ships like these could have gone south via a sea route. They needed a way to provision the Classis Germanica – the Roman military fleet moored on the Eastern Scheldt – from the north. Using inland waterways worked just fine. I think the canal must have extended all the way to the Scheldt. But as yet we haven't been able to prove it."

At the mouth of the canal, Hazenberg found a bronze mask of the kind worn by elite Roman cavalrymen at demonstrations and parades. Custom-made, it reveals something of the face that hid behind it: curly hair, prominent cheekbones, deep-set eyes, a thin mouth. If it's true there was a bridge over the canal at Fort Matilo, then the mask was probably an offering to the river god by a soldier grateful to be coming home in one piece, his curls now growing grey.

He was a Canninefate, a member of a small, coastal Germanic tribe that supplied the Roman army with two dozen cavalrymen every year in exchange for tax exemption and being left in peace. Twenty-five years of galloping in the service of the Romans ending in a little splash, a flash in the cloudy water, a ripple fanning out over the surface until finally it came to a halt against the indifferent hull of a moored barge.

And then the rest of life.

To ensure the men had no time on their hands, he dug a canal, twenty-three miles in length, between the Meuse and the Rhine, so the hazards of the ocean could be avoided.

From Annals XI, *Tacitus*

Fifteen years after Emperor Claudius had sent him to the mouth of the Rhine to chase off pirates, Gnaeus Domitius Corbulo – still alive, another emperor down the line – stood in front of his troops in Armenia. One of his many rivals, the senator and army commander Paetus, had surrendered to the Parthians in humiliating circumstances, and it was up to Corbulo to restore Rome's authority on the eastern border. He had dispatched the demoralised survivors of the Paetus fiasco to Syria, filling the gaps with seasoned troops, and was now about to address the reinforcements.

The men braced themselves; Corbulo liked to impress his authority by making examples. In Lower Germany he'd had two legionaries executed just for laying aside their swords while digging fortifications. A Roman soldier should be a fighting machine even when he was digging, even if it made work awkward.

There he stood, General Corbulo. Burly body, weathered face. The sun scorched his helmet, his cold eyes rested on his troops and the hairs of his helmet crest stood erect, as if on the back of an enraged animal. It was deathly still, even the crickets fell silent.

Then he started to shout. The oaths he unleashed on his troops – threatening them, cursing Paetus, yelling obscenities about the Parthians – were later delicately rephrased by Tacitus. "He spoke with great authority, which counted as eloquence in the military man."

He solved the Parthian problem. Five years later he committed suicide by order of Nero, exclaiming *"Axios!"* * as he fell on his own sword.

In AD 46 this same man, then a lot younger but no less fierce, had come down the Rhine to the North Sea. Five years had passed since his brother-in-law Caligula had been stabbed to death by his own elite guard. The change of power had been a perilous moment for Corbulo, but apparently the new emperor deemed him sufficiently *axios* to spare his life. He did send him far from Rome though, to Lower Germany, where the settlements behind the dunes were being harassed by a deserted soldier-turned-pirate. The Romans called him Gannascus the Canninefate, raised on a farm at the foot of dunes somewhere between the river mouths, not far from where The Hague stands now. The Canninefates were a tribe of farmers and fishermen, prosperous but small enough in number that they only had to supply two dozen men as auxiliaries for the Roman army. Those men would leave the farm, bound for faraway places: a posting on the Danube or in north Africa. A quarter of a century would pass before they could return to their spiritual home on the North Sea.

It was much too long for Gannascus. He preferred to fight, pillage and die in the place where he'd grown up, farms where the women who'd stayed behind ruled the roost. Most didn't follow their husbands to remote foreign postings, but chose to keep the farm running. They harvested peas, lentils and oats, and made enough cheese, butter and beer to barter with the Romans and lead a reasonably comfortable existence. The memories of their sons and husbands

* "I am worthy!"

being marched off faded. Now and then they'd get a sign of life from Britain, Thrace or Numidia: a couple of coins or two wooden tablets, nailed together, on which a message had been scratched. Many of the men who unexpectedly returned, half a lifetime later, turned out to be good-for-nothings who told rambling anecdotes, picked fights and cried out in their sleep. They spent the rest of their days in the inn, together with other veterans.

A mug's game, Gannascus thought. He loathed soldiering so much that after only a few years he reappeared at the farm on a moonless night. As a deserter he obviously he couldn't stay there – he himself realised that. On another dark night he pushed a dugout canoe into the water and vanished into the labyrinth of islands off the mouth of the Rhine. Within a few months he'd gained the confidence of the Chauci, who'd long dabbled in piracy around the river mouths. He joined them on raiding trips in the labyrinth of creeks between land and sea. They used dugout canoes made of oak tree trunks, paddled by a twenty-man crew across shallows where heavy Roman warships ran aground.

Until Corbulo arrived. Not two decades had passed since the Frisian revolt – less than a period of military service. Everyone could still remember it, and many who'd actually fought in the uprising were still alive to tell the tale. Romans were not invincible, they knew, and the Frisians, in their brackish wilderness above the river, had since been left in peace. The humiliation had not been avenged.

Moreover, the presence of the river, which even the Romans couldn't bridge or tame, created a kind of equality among the inhabitants of its banks. But acknowledging that the river is stronger than you, that there are forces more powerful than the will of Rome, that there are barbarians who derive their self-worth from that fact – to Corbulo, all this was completely unacceptable.

*

We know little or nothing about what the Canninefates called their children. Tacitus mentions the names of two insurgents: Brinno the rebel and Gannascus the pirate, though likely enough Gannascus wasn't his real name, but a Latin version of something like Gannasc. In Tipaza, a Roman fort on the coast of present-day Algeria, the gravestone has been found of a man called Adiutor, an equestrian in the first squadron of Canninefates, who died at the age of forty-six after twenty-three years of service – tantalisingly close to the prospect of Roman citizenship and of going home. His successor Cabanus, presumably a member of his tribe who also ended up in North Africa, erected the stone in his memory. Adiutor, a Latin word for "helper" or "auxiliary soldier", certainly wasn't his real name, though he might have been registered under it as a recruit.

But his image has been carved into the stone. A curly-haired cavalryman on a rearing horse; he looks valiant, his long lance is pointing forwards. His soldier's cape billows out behind him, showing how fast he's galloping. He's wearing close-fitting trousers and a loose tunic that puffs out over the belt around his middle. A piece of fabric hastily draped over the horse's back serves as an improvised saddle. Adiutor is portrayed as a spirited and accomplished horse-man who could ride at speed while brandishing a lance. His cape is of course held in place by a large, fine cloak pin on his right shoulder.

This is what the Canninefates could expect when, in

their early twenties, they were hauled off their farms: to be galloping along the peripheries of the empire in the service of Rome, unthinkably far from home.

That gives us Brinno, Gannascus, Adiutor and Cabanus, with Brinno actually being the only credible, non-Latinised Canninefate name. It was a small community, so he'd have been known to the farmer's wife who saw General Corbulo ride past her courtyard on a stormy day in the autumn of AD 48. The toddler she'd clutched by the collar, and who gazed up from the secure folds of her skirts at the horseman with his colourful cape, his sword, his mounted escort, had a name that sounded like Brinno. Of the West Germanic names that have been passed down to us there are a few that you can imagine the farmer's wife whispering to her child: "Stay here, Sicco, Baudulf, Atto, Vihirnas, Elzo, Dacco . . ." She would have been called Gannica, Pauta, Bertisindis, Roteldis, Duda . . .

He had curly hair, just like Adiutor, and he held on to his mother's skirts for reassurance, his little fists clenched tight. What happened next would stay with him for ever, even though he was only three years old at the time.

Corbulo reined in his horse and called out. A little further along, where hundreds of men had been busy for weeks digging a canal alongside the Vliet, two soldiers looked up. They were led to Corbulo, knelt down, the general yelled. Work stopped; the engineers, the hireling farm boys, the traders, everyone was rounded up and arranged to form three sides of a square, so they could all see what was to happen. The two arrested soldiers were made to stand up and strip off their clothes. One of the general's guards dismounted, drew his sword and stabbed the soldiers one after the other in the abdomen. They collapsed and died. Then Corbulo yelled a bit more. The toddler burst into tears. Corbulo turned round and looked at him, and then at his mother. She picked up the child and fled inside the farm.

The Canninefates knew why Corbulo was so touchy in those years. He'd killed Gannascus and he'd swept the north clean of pirates, but Claudius hadn't allowed him to cross the river, track the pirates to their own villages, kill them and burn their houses to the ground.

He was laughed at behind his back. Because he didn't avenge himself, because the Chauci pirates got away scot-free, and of course because he was the brother-in-law of the former emperor, of whom it was said that he'd sailed down a branch of the river to the sea, not so very far away, to dance on the beach and collect shells. Nobody had been there, no-one knew exactly what had happened, but it was a good story.

The Rhine was just like a bull, a two-horned god: every Roman knew that. The Canninefates lived in the region between the two horns. The canal that Corbulo had his men dig cut straight through the farmland bordering the dunes. Bisecting the Canninefates' fields, it created a navigational route from the northern to the southern branch of the Rhine, where the Roman North Sea fleet was based. Corbulo had dug the canal to show what he was capable of and to keep his soldiers out of mischief. Also to be able to crush rebellions faster and to provision the new fort Matilo – built where his canal branched off from the northern river towards the other estuary in the south – without having to travel by sea. Both estuaries discharged Rhine water, but the southern one was broader, because upstream it had been swelled by water from the Meuse.

The farmers who since time immemorial had punted their livestock along the meandering Vliet and held rowing races with dugout canoes were forced to witness how, in the space of a few months, their old creeks and streams were dredged, broadened and corralled into an arrow-straight waterway down which, in the years that followed, cargo ships over forty paces long, with billowing sails and ten oarsmen in the stern, reared up like stray monsters as they sailed through the fields. The flat vessels were loaded with pottery, grain, peat, timber, amphorae, bolts of fabric, and sometimes weapons and horses. Now and then, warships of even heavier draught passed by, the swelling sound of their drums heard above the larks, the rhythmic slap of oars on water, the bow like a swan's neck, a row of shields along the side.

Occasionally, when it had rained on the land of the Belgians and the Meuse was full, the water would flow through the canal from south to north. At other times, when a full moon and westerly storms created high water, causing the river to hesitate at its mouth, the water in the canal rose above the timbers of the embankment and flooded the surrounding land. But the water from the south and north mostly only rose a little at high tide. Day after day, the two small tidal waves collided gently in the middle, causing fine river sand to float to the bottom. So it didn't take long before warships began to run aground at that spot, and it had to be dredged.

The Romans did a lot of innovative, impressive things. But when stuck on a ship that's stranded in the middle of a canal, even the most heroic, well-armed soldiers look a bit pathetic and vulnerable.

*

By AD 67 the canal had become impassable. The toddler who witnessed the execution is now a man of twenty-two. His mother is getting on in years, his father is dead, he has married, and his wife has come to live with him on the farm. They have a one-year-old son, and the young man – let us call him Dacco, his wife Roteldis, and their son Gaisio – receives word that his name has been drawn and that he must report for military duty. He, of all his peers. He curses, kicks the milking stool, rushes out of the stall to his horse, jumps on her back and digs his heels in her flank. Her ears flattened, the horse bolts from the farmyard, clods of earth fly and the furious young farmer disappears along the cursed canal with its still water, the sun at his back. Chasing his shadow, he races as far as the river. Here, he stops. He screams across the water, at the Frisians who can stay home, he screams at the current that flows impassively towards the sea, and then he gallops further downstream, until the orchards become dunes and he hears the low rumble of the sea and his horse baulks. The river has widened, and in the fan of gullies is an archipelago of scattered banks, islands that impede a clear view of the sea. Willow trunks stuck into the water mark the deeper channel in which ships can sail upriver: occasional trading ships from the opposite shore, Roman warships. Gannascus and his pirates removed the trunks so that the ships would run aground. Gannascus who deserted the army, Gannascus whom they betrayed and tortured to death.

He turns and heads for home. The sun shines down upon him. Soldiers in the watchtowers of the Praetorium Agrippinae army camp see him approach. He is an outstanding horseman, an asset to the army.

That evening in the temple, he offers a sacrifice to the Triple Goddesses. They are carved into a vertical altar stone, seated next to one another, baskets of fruit on their laps, a dog sitting alongside them. They listen, they dispense Godspeed and protection to the fellow tribesmen who travel on the river or venture across the sea. Dacco and Roteldis are not the only ones. They offer red and black berries and apples. The apples are still green, but the goddesses acknowledge the gesture. They are a bit like all mothers, they see through our actions.

In a year's time, Emperor Nero will half-heartedly stab himself in the neck and unleash a civil war. Even though it yet hasn't come to this when Dacco leaves his farm at sunrise the next morning, things have already become restless in Gaul and the tension is palpable amongst the Batavians and along the canal. But Dacco has a wife, a child, a farm with cattle and some arable land, there are so many ways for the Romans to harm him, there is too much to lose, he sees no other choice than to leave his home close to the North Sea together with twenty-three comrades, heading first to Xanten, then to Moguntium (Mainz), finally joining his cavalry unit in Carnuntum, a large fort on the Danube just past Vindobona (Vienna). There he will be given a uniform and a horse, and the prospect of the long crossing to Numidia, the garrison of Tipaza, where the sea is crystal-clear, drinking water is scarce, and there is no such thing as winter. And so he disappears first from his and Roteldis' farm, then from the stories, then from her thoughts, and finally from her memory.

She could have gone with him, led a nomadic existence, lived in the villages outside the garrison, like at Matilo, where not only soldiers but women and children had come from all corners of the empire. But the Canninefate women stayed at home.

*

It is the spring of AD 93 when Dacco sails down the Rhine on a cargo ship, heading homewards. He has served his twenty-five years, he has been repeatedly elected *decurion*, leader of ten men, by his squadron; he has served on the Danube, in Numidia, and five years ago he was back on the Rhine, at Mainz, where Saturninus, the governor of Upper Germany, led an uprising against Emperor Domitian. Saturninus met a swift end: his army of rebels was surrounded on three sides, and because the ice on the Rhine suddenly thawed, the Chatti troops could not come to his aid. They stood on the wrong shore and watched the ice floes tumble over one another as they were carried off by the rushing meltwater.

When the fighting was over, Dacco stood on the shore and looked downstream and was, for the first time in years, overcome by homesickness. He had five years to go.

And now he is at the stern of a river ship loaded with building materials and glass, headed for Matilo and the settlement that is home to the temple of the Triple Goddesses and has been smartly renamed Municipium Aelium Canaefatium.

Shortly before his return, he knows, there had been a massive uprising against the Romans. Brinno had taken part. Matilo and Nigrum Pullum were razed. The rebels – Civilis and the Batavians – had got as far as Xanten. He had seen Civilis being dragged by a chariot through the streets of Rome. There was nothing left of him. They had fed him to the lions.

Then came the civil war, the three short-lived emperors Galba, Otho and Vitellius, and only when Vespasian, a swashbuckler from an equestrian family, took over did things settle down somewhat. Gradually, new tribesmen came as auxiliaries to Numidia. Roteldis was still alive, Dacco learned. The farm had suffered damage, but had been rebuilt. There were two barns now, and the harvest was good. There was something else, but they weren't sure how to tell him. Dacco raised his hands. "Enough," he said, "enough."

The long, flat boat bobs along with the current, the shore glides quickly past, it is a hot day, just as it was back then. A breeze picks up from the south, cows stand up to their bellies in the water. Now and then the sail flaps, but it is so quiet on board that one can hear the wind in the alder trees on the shore. A sound like spring rain.

This is the only thing he recognises; for the rest, everything he once knew has been swept away by the rebellion, or rebuilt, or transformed by time: different, bigger, indomitable, Roman.

As they approach Matilo, the oarsmen take up position at the stern. The sails are struck and the helmsman steers the ship to the calm shore of the river. There they turn, the sail is hoisted again and the oarsmen bring the ship into the canal. On the quay, young men stand ready to catch the hawsers. Dacco looks around, but recognises no-one. This was his world, he was taken from it, life has gone on without him.

He had to leave his uniform and his horse behind. All he has in his haversack is his full dress uniform, the one he wore on the parade grounds: like a barbarian, Far East horseman, without breastplate, his broad frame in tight-fitting trousers, a trim tunic and leather belt. He quickly rose in the army's ranks to a company of superior horsemen, whose parade dress includes a gilded helmet with yellow plume, the face hidden behind a bronze mask. They would charge the spectators like gods, swerve at the last moment, jump hurdles, feign jousting. Their clothing swirling with brightly coloured embroidery. He wore yellow, it became his colour, always had been, the yellow of the springtime flowers in his orchards. It's all in his haversack and he scans the quay and steps ashore. He has caught the villagers' attention, but still no-one recognises him. He crosses the swing bridge to his side of the canal and walks homewards.

The farm is small but prosperous. Roteldis is older than he had expected. She does not recognise him, but realises who he is. She has married his younger brother, who wasn't called up, who could stay at home. Of their four children, one is in the army, a bodyguard. Gaisio is dead. Drowned. It was an accident.

Dacco sits, stands up again.

That evening he and Roteldis go to the temple, bringing the same offering as before: berries and apples.

He says, "I don't know if I can ever come home."

She says, "I hope you understand."

"Of course." And then he says, "I'm still here – have a feel."

Back at home, he removes the mask from his haversack, holds it up to his face to scare his nephews. The dog barks at him, the boys whoop. Then Dacco nods to his brother, as if to remind him of an old understanding, and he and Roteldis go out to walk along the canal, down to the river. Dusk has already fallen. She walks at some distance from him.

She says, "I still have to get used to this."

He says, "The world is so much bigger than you can imagine."

And when they reach the river, he says, "There are rivers much wider than ours. But we belong here. I want to come back, because I ached for home, even though nothing I knew is left."

He brings out the mask that concealed his face during his most glorious moments and says, "Since I'm still alive, and we are lost without the gods, and time has passed without us knowing it, I want you to return this mask to where it came from."

Roteldis takes it from him, together they walk onto the bridge that crosses the mouth of the canal where it meets the river. In the falling darkness and while reciting a prayer, she drops the mask into the water.

They look down. A splosh, ripples on the water's surface, a few air bubbles, and it is gone.

Supposed "experts" had convinced the king that it was possible to sail comfortably from the Danube to the Rhine if a navigable canal was dug between the rivers Rednitz and Altmühl, because the one flowed to the Main and the other to the Danube.

From Annales regni Francorum *(Royal Frankish Annals)*

It is the year 803 and Charlemagne, or Charles the Great, is standing in Mainz on the bank of the Rhine. He looks across the water, where a new church dedicated to the Holy Redeemer has been erected alongside the ruins of the Roman Castellum. Next to him is his diminutive shadow, the scholar Einhard.

Charlemagne might tower above other men, but not in a freakish way. Later, Einhard would describe the emperor as tall, but not disproportionately so, his height being seven times the length of his own foot. Modern-day research of Charlemagne's left tibia has shown him to be 1.84 metres, or six feet, tall.

So, tall, yes, but not a beanpole or a giant. Tall enough to literally look down upon his subjects, Einhard in particular, who was himself small of stature. "His height was contemptible," observed a certain Walahfrid, a contemporary of Einhard.

They watch as a ferry crosses the river bearing the body of Ada, a well-to-do woman from Mainz whose aunt had had the church built twenty-five years earlier. Her coffin lies on a soberly decorated bier, to which four impatient horses are tethered. Their ears flat, they eye the water that flows below them. It is springtime and the river is high. Upstream, it has rained for days on end. The ferry, attempting to maintain its decorum during the crossing, struggles against the force of the river, which wants to drag the deceased further downstream to where the heathens live.

The ferry is operated by a chain attached to the remains of the Roman pilings. Emperor Charlemagne, the bishop, the nobles of Mainz and the villagers further along the riverbank watch and hold their breath. Representatives of the Abbey of Fulda, across the river, likewise watch nervously.

There hasn't been a bridge over the Rhine for some four hundred years. The Roman bridge here at Mainz was destroyed, possibly burned down when the Vandals and Alemanni attacked on New Year's Eve in the year 406. It was one of the few bridges the Romans built over the Rhine. The flat, fertile land on the eastern shore was vulnerable. Hence a well-stocked garrison in Mainz, and an outpost in a *castellum* on the enemy side.

But that was more than four centuries ago. What is left of the Roman infrastructure, overgrown and decrepit, is scattered across the southern and western regions of Charlemagne's territory. He has done his best to tackle some of this ramshackle legacy, but there is only so much one emperor can do in a lifetime.

So there they stand, the exalted monarch and his puny scholar, gazing out over the river. They watch as the ferry approaches the far shore. Charlemagne is recognisable only by his height and his entourage; he is otherwise dressed in modest Frankish attire, leather straps criss-crossing his calves, his belly jutting out under his linen shirt. He has long silver hair, ditto beard. A massive sword hangs motionless at his side.

The ferry reaches calmer waters and moors safely on the far bank. The tension on this side ebbs, the men laugh with relief. Einhard peers across the water at the men from Fulda: perhaps he'll recognise someone from his days at the monastery school. Abbot Baugulf had seen his talent, sent him to study at the court school in Aachen, instructed him to do his best and to visit now and again. But Abbot Baugulf was deposed last year and banished to the Wolfmünster monastery. He had taken too many liberties, his followers said.

Einhard tries to make out faces. Perhaps Ratgar, the architect who is now abbot, will be at the funeral. They say he rules with an iron hand. Einhard remembers him well from his school days. They used to speculate on how to build the biggest churches, how to roof over the heavens. How slender could an arch be? A church mustn't be some tenebrous fortress, but a light, elegantly structured space.

"God is great," Einhard often remarked, pointing to a sketch for a large-scale design.

"Yes, and man is small," Ratgar would reply, and push Einhard over.

Nasty Ratgar, never even good for a laugh.

Einhard eyes the spot where the Main flows into the Rhine. There, near that tributary, he was born. Charlemagne looks down at him, reads his thoughts.

"Close to home," he remarks. Einhard cocks his head, listens. Charlemagne has the soft-spokenness of one whose word is law.

"There used to be a bridge here," the emperor continues. He sees Einhard survey the pilings. "Rebuild it."

The urban elites standing behind them shift restlessly, glance nervously at one another, then at the river. Charlemagne turns to them. "Einhard will instruct you further." The men are taken aback, but they bow. Einhard draws the Mainz leaders to one side.

"It will be costly," he says, "but not only for you." He nods towards the other side, where the funeral procession makes its way up the riverbank. "For them, too."

The ferry sails back across the water, moors a little later on their side. The company follows the emperor down to the river's edge.

A few years later, carts rattle over the wooden structure. The metal wheel rims spark against the nails. The burghers of Mainz walk out onto the bridge, look down at the ships that pass under the arches. The skippers strike their masts, look up suspiciously. They feel vulnerable, and they are.

In 813 the wooden structure again goes up in flames – the blame was put on bandits who beset the ships from the bridge. Charlemagne is in Aachen now, he is overweight, his speech is slurred and he drags one leg. He takes hot baths, but it doesn't help: he's lost all feeling in that leg.

He dies a year later.

*

Einhard stays on at the royal court, in the service of Charlemagne's son Louis. Now that Charlemagne is dead, the idea takes hold to write his life story, as Suetonius did with *The Twelve Caesars*. Not as a historical chronicler, but as a biographer of the man himself, his legacy. A book describing not only his deeds, his conquests and his administration, but also a more personal account of the man: the sound of his voice, how he spent his days, how he dressed, what he liked to eat, how just, temperate, resolute, amiable, wise – in short, how wonderful he was. So Einhard erected, in words, a monument to a great man with a round head, large and lively eyes, a big nose, silver hair, a bright and

cheerful expression, a short, fat neck, firm belly, modest
Frankish attire and a soft voice. Temperate with drink but
enamoured of roast game and hunting.

To refresh his memory, Einhard turns to chronicles
written by court writers who meticulously recorded the
deeds and events at the Frankish court. He pages through
these accounts, vexed at times by the verbose style and the
inaccuracies, then searches further, toying with the idea of
rewriting the whole thing himself but, realising he hasn't
much time, skims on.

Not everything he reads is suitable for inclusion in his
biography. But the construction of the royal chapel in
Aachen, the fort in Nijmegen, the palace at Ingelheim, and
of course the bridge at Mainz – these must go in. Not only
because he, as court architect, had a hand in it. The praise
is due the emperor and the emperor alone. Everyone knows,
after all, that none of it would have been built without his,
Einhard's, contribution.

Einhard arrives at the first years of his tenure at court.
791: the campaign against the Avars, the march along the
Danube. Charlemagne, still merely king back then, returns
triumphantly to Regensburg to spend the winter. 792:
Einhard reads the sparse reports (there were no military
campaigns that year) and thinks, "What about all that
palaver with the Spanish?"

This had been his first whole calendar year at the court.
He remembers his own journey to Regensburg, where
he saw how the courtiers, in the absence of a military campaign, got themselves worked up over the heresy of a certain
Spanish bishop, Felix van Urgell. This Felix preached that
Christ was a man of flesh and blood, and an adopted, rather
than the true son of God. Felix was summoned from the

Pyrenees to Regensburg, where Charlemagne and a handful of outraged bishops hauled him over the coals; his stubbornness got him sent on to Rome, where, having to face the Holy Father, he temporarily sublimated his heretical thoughts.

Einhard reads and recalls the furore. He remembers the know-alls surrounding Charlemagne and their flim-flam, and how impressed he, a young courtier, was with all of it. He remembers thanking God in his evening prayers for having landed at the epicentre of the Christian world, that he, within earshot of God Himself, was witness to passionate deliberations concerning truth and eternity.

During the many banquets that year he heard ever taller tales of the previous year's campaign against the Avars; how the king's army advanced: the king himself on the south bank of the Danube, the Frisian and Saxon mercenaries on the north bank, and the ships with supplies and troops in the middle of the river. That the sight of Charlemagne's approach alone had the Avars quaking in their boots. Imagine the impression it would have made, then, said one of the battle's veterans, if the king's Rhine warships could have been there, too.

Roars from the men, fists thumping the tabletop.

Everyone knew it was impossible, unless the ships were carried across land from the one river to the other. Charlemagne, whose realm included numerous waterways (from the Elbe in the north to the Tiber in the south, and from the Loire in the west to the Danube in the east), had to keep all his fleets in service to maintain his power. Even though they were under the command of the holiest of kings, there was no way they would or could be consolidated.

This uncomfortable notion, coupled with the overconfidence and the boredom of Regensburg, combined to bring forth the plan to dig a canal between the Danube and the Main, a branch of which (near Weißenburg) came within two thousand paces of the Danube.

"Can it be done?" Charlemagne asked no-one in particular.

"You can do anything," replied an army engineer confidently. The table cheered in approval. The emperor scowled: he could not abide drunkards.

Einhard turns the page to the year 793, where the chronicle tells of Charlemagne travelling to the west to view the trench between the Danube and the Main. He knows for certain that this passage needs editing. By now everyone knows that this project was a disaster, that the canal, never used, is silting up. It must be made clear, once and for all, that it was not Charlemagne's error, that canal, but his advisers', the company of counsellors to which Einhard, a newcomer, had not yet been admitted.

This episode of the canal is not going into Charlemagne's biography at all.

The memory of his stay in Weißenburg is that it was dark and unpleasant. Einhard saw for the first time how thousands of men were dragged away from their labours or farms to work on it, and how the region came undone; how the digging operations began but were hampered by constant rain; how the monarch gradually realised what a shambles the project had become, and that he received nothing but bad news from the outside: treason in the north, incursions in the south. Charlemagne left Weißenburg and the work ground to a halt.

Einhard beckons a scribe, he points to the half-empty page at the year 793, and says, "Write this down":

Supposed "experts" had convinced the king that it was possible to sail comfortably from the Danube to the Rhine if a navigable canal was dug between the rivers Rednitz and Altmühl, because the one flowed to the Danube and the other to the Main. Thus he travelled at once, with his whole entourage, to that spot, recruited a great number of men, and devoted the entire autumn to this project. A canal was dug between the rivers, two thousand paces long and three hundred feet wide. But it was for naught: ceaseless rainfall and the marshy ground meant that what the diggers excavated during the day simply slid back at night to where it had come from.

*

In the pavement of Weißenburg's market square is a marker indicating the outer boundary of the Roman *limes* fort Biriciana, on which the town was founded. A few metres further is another marker indicating the edge of the Frankish settlement where Charlemagne had lived during the construction of the canal. The market square is oblong, lined with half-timbered houses with steep-sloped or bell gables and a Gothic town hall at one end. In 793, when he arrived, the spot already had houses and workshops that looked out onto one another.

The emperor slept, ate and received his exhausted messengers a few streets further up, in a solid-looking house on the spot where the church of St Andreas now stands.

Nowhere does the town mention Charlemagne's attempt to dig the canal. There is a statue in the market square, but it is of one King Ludwig of Bavaria, who gave Weißenburg its municipal charter in the fourteenth century. He leans nonchalantly on his shield, right leg rigid and left relaxed, as though to spread the weight of his crown, pauldrons and coat of mail. He looks downwards with a slight frown. Something is clearly bothering him. Beneath his feet, a fountain gurgles. A statue that makes you want to pee.

Weißenburg is situated on the Rhine side of the Danube. The Schwabian Rezat (which Einhard calls the "Rednitz") flows past the town, heading slowly to the Main in the north, where Charlemagne had to unload his ships and transport the freight across the watershed to the next river.

Place of discontent, place of delays.

Charlemagne is forgotten here. Apparently the city would rather not be associated with the canal that went down in history as an utter failure. Just to the south, in the town of Graben, it is otherwise. There, a few hundred metres of the canal between the Rhine and the Danube have been re-dug. A cluster of well-illustrated information panels explains it in detail. A nearby barn houses a small museum, open in high season.

The newly dug canal cuts through a hill marking the watershed between the Rhine and the Danube. On the northern side, the rainwater flows via the Rezat to the Main; on the southern side, via the Altmühl to the Danube.

This dead-end waterway glides amongst the trees, tranquil as a forest brook. The treetops meet halfway across the water, like a gateway, as tall as a cathedral. The shorelines are steep and show traces of erosion – a sure sign that, if left to their own devices, they would collapse back into the water just like in that wet autumn of 793.

A fresco on the side of a building next to the information

panels shows a trio of diggers excavating a path from the mermaid of the Danube to Rhenus, the god of the Rhine, who looks a lot like Neptune. Each mythical figure hovers above their own river, the water gushes around them, over-sized fish leap about. Rhenus, entwined with grapevines, holds a goblet of wine. The mermaid wears a medium-length dress that reaches halfway down her tail.

High up on the banks of the canal is a walking path that looks down through the trees to the dark water. The canal's grandeur fades the further you go. Buckled trees lie with their crowns submerged, roots sticking out of the water. The only footbridge over the canal has collapsed from wood rot. The structure's remains are cordoned off with red and white tape, like a crime scene.

The canal, by this time, has narrowed to a muddy stream, half overgrown with brambles. After just a kilometre, all that's left of Charlemagne's canal is a ditch that stops dead at a railway embankment.

One of the houses along the railway tracks also sports a brightly coloured fresco showing Charlemagne inspecting the excavation; each leg bound with leather straps, billowing tunic. In front of the house, a small monument has been erected, a stone pillar informing the passer-by that this is the spot where the waters of the Rhine and the Danube part company. Some water trickles out of the monument; there is a small warning sign: KEIN TRINKWASSER. The water runs off on the Danube side and into the ground.

There's Rhenus and the Danube nymph again in one of the reliefs carved into the stone. They shake hands over a low wall. The mermaid has exchanged her fish body for a pair of naked human legs. Her lower body is draped nonchalantly with a shawl, which mostly – but not entirely – covers her buttocks. She looks guardedly, a little darkly, at the hand-shake. Father Rhine's grapevines have slipped down to his loins. He appears to have been caught out, embarrassed, and not quite sure where to look.

The northern end of the canal once lay on the other side of the railway tracks. After a bit of searching, I identify the course by the remains of an earthen embankment running through a field with a fringe of reeds along its base. It has started to rain, the reeds rustle gently. After standing there for a while, I notice that the rainwater running off my jacket has collected in a puddle around my shoes, and is flowing away from me. I follow the little stream, parallel to the reed fringe. It creeps to the edge of the field, where it trickles into a brooklet. The water gurgles on its way to the North Sea.

ISLANDS

As deacon Accola of Flims so aptly put it in his eulogy, onlookers would often break into a cold sweat at the sight of Stury, grasping the steel cable, sweeping across the Rhine.

From a local obituary on the death of Josef Anton Stury-Camenisch, the "Robinson of the Rhine"

When the last ice age was over and glaciers in the Alps receded from the lower mountain valleys, the rock faces they left behind needed another couple of thousand years to sweat out all the permafrost that had nestled into their cracks and fissures. In the Rhine valley between Ilanz and Reichenau, that meltwater had a long way to go. The glacier that had crept through the valley for a hundred thousand years had pushed against the mountain slopes with unimaginable force, displacing and splitting rocks as much as hundreds of metres below the surface. The fissures that had worked themselves deep into the mountain were filled all the way to their capillaries: an icy root system that held the mountain together like a clod of dirt.

But with the glacier's retreat, the ice water seeped out of the mountain, drop by drop, in the ever warmer summers until it lost its grip on the mountain. One day, 9,450 years ago, the cracked and tormented mountain imploded, collapsing with a mighty crash. More than ten cubic kilometres of broken rock slid down the hillside. An unfathomably violent avalanche that filled the Rhine valley with a mountain of rubble hundreds of metres high and thirteen kilometres long.

But the Rhine is patient. Its waters, whose course had been dammed off by the avalanche, formed a lake further upstream that in a matter of years filled the entire valley. The water pushed at the blockade with burgeoning force. Ever so gradually, the boulders shifted, took smaller ones with them, let water through, rolled further. More than fifteen hundred winters of freeze and thaw broke and crumbled the boulders into football-sized rocks, pebbles and sand. The Rhine water that flowed over the edge of the dam gouged itself a bed, and the Alpine Rhine slowly resumed its path.

That's how the Rheinschlucht, the Rhine Gorge, came into being: a canyon thirteen kilometres long, with cliffs that rise up over three hundred metres. These days, you can watch the water gush over rocks and pebbles, or slow down, churning in deep, turquoise pools. The grey-white walls of what was once the mountain tower above the river, which here and there curves around a stubborn remnant of the landslide jutting out from the steep mountainside like a small peninsula.

On one of these peninsulas, "Isla Casti", lived a carpenter, his seven children and his uncomplaining wife, cut off from the rest of the world. The man, who died in 1970 at the age of eighty-five, was named Josef Anton Stury, and his wife was Anna Margaretha Camenish. Stury was a resourceful eccentric who only reluctantly left the island to sell trout in the nearby towns of Flims and Versam and take on the occasional carpentry job. The farmers and villagers kept their distance; they nicknamed him "the Robinson of the Rhine."

The river at that point is between only ten and twenty metres wide, but it is still too rough and too cold to wade through or swim across. There is no bridge to Isla Casti, so Stury lived with his wife, children and goats on this isolated patch of land in the river as a sort of "mountain islander". The fact that it's technically a peninsula in no way diminished their isolation. The cliff to which Isla Casti is attached rises more than a sheer hundred metres. When he was young and limber, it took Stury more than two hours to clamber up it. Once on top, it was another hour's walk through the woods to the town of Flims. When he got older, he just stayed down below.

Stury, born in 1885, fought for Germany in World War I on the Russian Front. After the war, he wanted nothing more to do with the rest of the world. He settled on Isla Casti, chopped down half of the trees, used the rushing river water to drive a sawmill, and with the resulting planks and beams he built himself a house. Meanwhile he regularly impregnated his wife Anna, and nine months later helped with the delivery. If the baby survived, he would hike up the cliff and return the next day with a goat to provide milk for the child. A cow would not have survived the descent.

Anna and Josef home-schooled their children until the education authorities in Graubünden convinced them to send their brood to school. Stury grudgingly strung a cable across the river to a rock on the opposite shore. He attached a leather saddle to a pulley, hung it on the cable, and henceforth on schooldays his seven children ziplined across the water, one at a time. In the afternoon they returned in the same manner, one by one. If the water was high, it spattered against their bottoms.

At night, in the bedsteads their father built, they would listen to the roaring river and the bleating of the restless goats. The Rhine, which embraced the island like a parent and held the world at bay, could suddenly transform into an angry monster that threatened to drown her own children. On one particularly violent September night, it slammed away almost ten acres of ground. By morning, the place where the goats grazed, the children played along the river and Stury fished for trout had been turned into a wasteland of rubble. The river gushed over uprooted trees, the grassland had vanished.

Before dinner that evening, Stury read the children the Biblical story of the Red Sea that deluged the Egyptians.

"We are still here," he explained. "Water destroys only its enemies."

Then came the prayers. Nine bowed heads above the dining table, nine pairs of folded hands, the knuckles white. Outside, the familiar whoosh of the river that drowned out the litany. At bedtime, father did a round of the bedsteads.

"The island is the most beautiful spot on earth," he said. "The Rhine is our father. We will never leave here."

But eventually everyone leaves. Stury, too. There are grainy film images, made in the late sixties with an 8-mm camera. He's a lean old man with a wispy beard and a churchwarden pipe. He shuffles around his island, wobbling against a walking stick, a smile on his face, goats at his side. A benign, somewhat wary old fellow, in clothes that did not shrink along with him, his baggy trousers hitched up at the back with braces.

"My ancestors were Greek fishermen," he says somewhere in the film. A year later, he was dead.

It was around this time that recreational kayak and canoe rentals first appeared on the Rhine. Tourists bundled up against the chill looked upon the shore of Isla Casti as they paddled past, and were in turn observed by Stury's goats and children. Hikers on the far bank would reach for the pulley, clearly hoping to cross via the cable to the other side.

For the young Sturys, the world was getting too close for comfort. They conferred, crossed to the other side, and came back with puppies under their jackets. They put them in cages, turned them vicious, and let them free come nightfall. The dogs roamed the property like a pack of angry wolves. On the far side, where the cable was attached, the children hung warning signs: no trespassing, beware of guard dogs. No-one tried to reach Isla Casti after that.

At the top of the cliff, an observation platform juts out, allowing tourists to look down the hundred-metre drop to the meandering river and Stury's island. I was there in the summer of 2019. A kindly Swiss woman named Beatrice had told me about the platform and Isla Casti, where the Robinson of the Rhine had lived. We walked there together, stepped out onto the platform, and looked down for a while.

"There's a new owner now," she said, "but he doesn't live there all year round. He was here recently to look for his cat, which had wandered off the island, and he told me about what happened to Stury's wife and children."

Twenty years after Stury's death, a helicopter flew down into the canyon to remove his elderly wife, who stubbornly refused to leave. In the end, the police evacuated the island.

"The family had become a bit crazy and violent," Beatrice said. "After the generator broke down for the third time, the wife and one of the daughters pretty much cracked. They needed help, had to be got off the island, but there was no reasoning with them. They were quite aggressive. The police had to first render the dogs harmless, then they airlifted the wife and daughter to a sanatorium. The women eventually recuperated."

We look down. You can clearly see the roof of the

abandoned wooden house. "Later, the children sold the island to someone who promised to keep it more or less the way it was. That was the guy with the cat. He said he planned to live there in the summer, but that the winters would be too much for him. That the river did strange things with your mind."

Beatrice looked down again. The rush of the water echoed up from the valley, blended with a gust of wind that whooshed across the treetops.

"Stury was a carpenter," she said. "A cabinetmaker. I've got a cupboard he made. Would you like to see it?"

We left the platform and walked to her house, a wooden chalet with geraniums on the balcony. She went inside and came out with a photo of the cupboard. It was nothing special, though very neatly finished. The door opened and closed easily, she said, and when it was shut you could hardly see the join.

"So this is his handiwork," Beatrice said. "*Der Stury.*"

I looked at the picture of the cupboard, as though that would explain everything. But it didn't, of course, and then we just kind of stood there, because we didn't know what else to do.

Food and drink made him nauseous, and he suffered from shortness of breath. Robbed of his strength, he decreed that a summer residence be built for him on an island across from the city of Mainz, and there he kept to his bed.

From The Life of Emperor Louis the Pious, *by an anonymous author nicknamed "The Astronomer"*

Drogo was out fishing when the news reached him that his brother, the pious emperor Louis, was dying. It was the spring of the year AD 840, the weather had just turned favourable for fishing. The evening air was warm and the water of the Moselle still cool, and insects danced above the sluggish current under the bridge outside the port. Although Drogo was bishop of Metz, he could often be found early in the morning and at dusk on the riverbanks, divested of his habit, distinguishable from an everyday Frank only by the ring of St Arnulf on his middle finger.

"St Peter was also a fisherman," he would say to anyone he saw scowl.

They can drop dead, he thought to himself.

Drogo was just thirty-eight when the herald from Ingelheim-upon-Rhine came to tell him his brother was gravely ill and had called for him. His half-brother Louis, the emperor they called "the Pious".

Drogo was used to his older brother needing him. When their father died and he went to Aachen to join Louis, his life changed overnight. He was just twelve, a child, but Louis quickly banished him from the court and thus from a secular life in which one married, waged war and went out fishing with friends at the day's end. Louis, twenty-one years older and Drogo's legal guardian, decided, now that he was emperor, that the young half-brother was a threat.

Away with him.

Louis had them shave the boy's curly locks into a tonsure, turning him into a harmless novice monk. He could become a royal cleric, pray for the souls of the family, hear confession, mollify potential rivals.

The hand that had hoped for a sword now wielded a staff, and sometimes a fishing rod. And producing offspring legally was out of the question. Drogo himself was a bastard, the son of Charlemagne's concubine Regina.

The messenger rode up the Hill of the Basilicas to summon the bishop.

"Monseigneur has gone fishing, outside the gate," they told him. A servant, familiar with the best place to catch bass, ran ahead. The tired steed's hoofbeats echoed off the houses in the narrow streets. Drogo was outside the gate, under the rattly planks of the bridge. He made the messenger kneel, his right knee in the mud of the riverbank.

"So. It's time, then," he said.

At the first light of dawn he left on horseback over the old Roman road to Trier, and from there on to Mainz. He rode without a break, galloped where possible. The messenger, who had not quite caught his breath after the previous day, did his best to keep up with him. It was not concern that spurred Drogo on. It was an overwhelming feeling of joy. He tried to justify this as reverently as possible, but there was no other way to describe it. His only worry was that he would arrive too late.

"His Highness has retired to the hunting lodge on the island off Ingelheim," the messenger said when they stopped in Trier for fresh horses. Drogo made him repeat it. Upon realising he had heard it right, Drogo laughed.

"Like a monk retreating from the world," he said to the messenger, who did not understand his joviality. On his way to eternal bliss, the pious emperor, he thought, on his own Lindisfarne, but out of reach of the Vikings.

"I take it His Highness is frequently at prayer?"

"He has stopped eating," replied the messenger. "Only the blood and the body of the Lord. But he spews that up, too."

Drogo nodded, mounted his horse and dug in his heels. He had more haste than he had thought.

Evening had fallen when he arrived at the palace of Ingelheim. The island lay broad and densely wooded in the river. In the palace he changed out of his travelling clothes into something more bishoply and was soon standing upright, like God's own scout, on the ferry that rowed him out to the island. The trees were already silhouettes against the approaching night, like a wall enclosing nothing but darkness. Behind that wall, he knew, was Louis.

On the shore of the island, alongside a creek that disappeared into the trees, men stood waiting with torches to aid the ferryman in his crossing. The oars sploshed in the black water. It occurred to Drogo that his brother, on that island, was already halfway to the other side, as though to meet a high-level emissary of a visiting king. He always strove to draw nearer to God, was always conscious of his guilt – as though that consciousness made any difference.

A gust of wind rushed through the trees and passed overhead. The current resisted, the oarsmen groaned. He instinctively scanned the treelined shore for a good place to fish.

Night had well and truly fallen by the time they arrived.

It was fearfully dark, the Rhine burbled, and the horses, spooked by the torches and by the night, refused to budge. So the company proceeded on foot. The torchlight made their shadows dance on the tree trunks and exposed roots along the path. It was a half-hour walk, they picked their way cautiously down the uneven forest path. The water in the creek gurgled and lapped alongside them, but eventually branched off so the only sound left was their footsteps and the rustling of the trees.

A pale habit appearing out of the darkness, like a ghost – thus did Drogo arrive at his brother's deathbed. Louis lay on his pillows, emaciated, his forehead drenched and his eyes ablaze. His hand clawed at Drogo's. He whispered something unintelligible.

Drogo turned to those in the room. "Whoever wishes to petition or address the emperor, shall do so through me," he said. "For now, leave us alone." He continued to look around until he was sure everyone had gone. Then he turned to his brother.

"You wish to confess, I am certain," he said. "Whisper it, or just think it, words no longer matter. God's mercy does not need the spoken voice. I know you, your broken spirit, your penitent heart."

In the hours that followed, they were closer to one another than ever before. The helpless emperor and his twenty-three-year younger half-brother.

Drogo had once been his ward, then his rival, and after Louis had reconciled with him, his spiritual guide. He became Louis' middleman, mediating between him and his legitimate sons, and between him and God. And now he was fulfilling his final role, that of priest who was to guide him into eternity. Louis' mouth gasped like a fish on dry land, his lips cracked. Drogo nodded and closed his eyes so as not to let on that he did, after all, have to force back tears. Outside the window, wild boars grubbed in the dirt, the sound of their snorting reached the deathbed.

By dawn, Louis had fallen asleep. Drogo left the room, asked the bishops Hetti of Trier and Otgar of Mainz to keep watch over the emperor, and walked out into the morning. He sought and found the messenger who had fetched him from Metz, instructing him to go back to the mainland and find a carpenter to build a coffin in which to take his brother off the island when the time came. Drogo saw the blood drain from his face. He blessed him, and said, "It's all right, kiss my ring, and hurry."

Then he took off his habit and walked away from the hunting lodge, over the gravel along the riverbank. The blue-green water gushed past where the creek that bisected the island met the river, he turned left and disappeared among the trees. The low morning sun drew stripes through the woods and shone onto the limpid water streaming under the leafy canopy. Drogo's eyes sparkled as he saw shoals of young fish in the sandy shallows, warming themselves in the morning sun. Gleaming purple dragonflies grazed the water's surface, and out of the corner of his eye he caught sight of a kingfisher who, in a flash of blue, darted from a branch into the water. He looked around, passed water into the creek, and sat down on a fallen tree trunk.

He thought of his brother and how he, Drogo, could both credit and blame him for everything he had become. When Louis had ordered that their cousin Bernard, who for some reason harboured a grudge against the emperor and conspired against him, should have his eyes put out, from which he died two excruciating days later, Louis had moved heaven and earth to make his remorse known to the world. He summoned bishops to his palace in Attigny and even invited His Holiness Pope Pascal, and spent many hours kneeling at the feet of the bishop of Rome.

What began as a confession of his harsh punishment of Bernard escalated into a litany of various lesser sins: fits of anger, the execution of enemies, evil thoughts, debauchery. The bishops exchanged glances, the pope tried to interrupt and get him to halt his keening. His sons Lothar and Louis raised their eyes heavenwards, and watched as their kneeling, snivelling father's dignity crumbled with each new peccadillo, until it was no longer an emperor prone there on the floor but a wad of pious parchment, a beaten dog.

Drogo witnessed it all and now, a few hundred paces removed from his dying brother, he still cannot decide which was stronger: his shame on his brother's behalf, his anger, his fear or his contempt. When Louis got up and begged him, too, for forgiveness, offering him to make him a cardinal, he hastened to reassure him. Anything, as long as the whimpering stopped.

That he would wear the cassock on which his brother depended for his own conscience – his brother the traitor, whom he despised and in spite of everything still loved – went some way to soften the agony, but did not quench it altogether.

Louis lingered at death's door. He confessed to Drogo every day, he swallowed the communion wafer but vomited it back up half an hour later. Drogo soothed him, advised him to make peace with the life he had led and with his approaching death, and with his sons, who hated him and were waiting eagerly for news of his demise.

When Louis' final day arrived, and he could move only his eyebrows and his fingers, Drogo performed Mass in the presence of all the religious emissaries in that cramped room. The end came suddenly. Drogo was reciting his Latin text when Louis, as though struck by lightning, bolted half-upright, stared in mortal terror at a dark corner of the room and shouted, hoarsely yet clearly, "Huz! Huz!" as though to chase away demons. As the others all turned to see what the emperor had shouted at, he fell back upon his pillow and his face broke into a smile. This is how he died. It was the twentieth of July.

Louis' body was laid in the opportunely delivered coffin and carried to the ferry. As he was rowed across the water that evening, off his island, a flock of gulls circled overhead. They hardly beat their wings, gliding around one another as though in a slow-motion cyclone travelling downstream. Drogo looked up and watched them until they were out of sight.

Drogo lived for another fifteen years. He drowned while fishing. His body was pulled out of the water and interred near his brother's, on the holy hill high above the Moselle in Metz.

RIVER SWIMMING

Am Rhein geboren
den Kampf mit dem Rhein hat sie verloren.

Plaque on the Old Rhine Bridge in Rheinfelden

When my aunt Ida told me that my father, her elder brother, had learned to swim in the Rhine, I could hardly believe my ears. That's because her memories evoked powerful and horrifying images: a film that our teacher, Master Wes, had shown us in class. It was my last year in primary school, 1973–74. The film drove home to me and my classmates the dire state of the river. The sombre fate of the Rhine, moreover, was a microcosm of the state of the world as a whole. Basically, we were all going to hell in a handcart.

Etched most of all in my memory was the underwater footage of a dying salmon in the murky, polluted Rhine water. The culprits, we learned, were the potassium mines in the Alsace and factories like BASF in Ludwigshafen. The film showed belching smokestacks that blocked out the setting sun and huge sewage pipes disgorging slimy, steaming and weirdly coloured wastewater into the river. Frothy water, poison, fumes, dead birds. The Rhine was an open sewer, a ceaseless source of toxins that polluted our country and our drinking water. And the French and Germans didn't give a damn.

The classroom was silent when the film finished. Heavy curtains blocked out the afternoon light, and in the darkness we sat there trying to digest what we'd just seen. The only sound was the flapping of the loose end of the film reel. Until someone asked the teacher if there was a Laurel & Hardy we could watch.

There was.

The mood improved at once. Especially when Master Wes ran the film again, this time at double speed and in reverse. When the bell went and the classroom emptied, I asked him if he had showed us the Rhine film so that, later, we might do something about it. He smiled and nodded.

So those images, especially of that salmon, were revived when I heard that my father had learned to swim in the Rhine. I was convinced that simply jumping into the Rhine would be as lethal as it had been for that fish. Later, in high school, this notion was confirmed by our biology teacher, Mr Suister. "Anyone who tries to swim across the Rhine has a death wish," he said. He, too, smiled as he said it.

I recently asked my aunt whether she remembered any of the details of those swimming lessons. What she told me conjured up a pre-war, black-and-white world, a pastoral river landscape with wheatfields and cows, a bicyclist on his way somewhere, a man in the prime of his life. My grandfather.

"Your granddad took me to the swimming place on the back of his bike," my aunt said. "Along the Kersweg and the Veerweg, as far as the ferry at Eck en Wiel, then you'd go left about two hundred metres along a small dyke, and there it was. With changing cabins and a ticket window. Just like a real swimming pool."

My aunt likes reminiscing, but she didn't understand my special interest in their swimming lessons. Up- and downstream there were plenty more Rhine pools: Wijk bij Duurstede, Elst, Renkum, Wageningen and Arnhem all had one, and this was just the Lower Rhine. Twenty kilometres south of that was the Meuse, the river in which my mother-in-law had apparently learned to swim when she was small, and where one can now swim again. So my father's swimming lessons weren't so unusual after all, but during the half-century surrounding my childhood, the river was so polluted that no-one in their right mind went in the water.

The Rhine pool, my aunt told me, was roped off with cork buoys, and it was where schoolchildren from Leersum and Amerongen went for swimming lessons, or just for recreation. Milk-white arms and legs, swimsuit tugged way up the belly. Bare feet sunk into the sand, toes getting cut on stones and shells. In the middle of the river, barge engines thumped and their chimneys smoked, but on the shore, the voice of the lifeguard echoed above it all. He was named Walboom, but good-humouredly endured the nickname Poolie. He wore white trousers and a cap. He was in his mid-thirties.

"Daredevils who thought they were good swimmers would duck under the ropes," my aunt told me. "They would drift downstream to the ferry and wait until a tugboat came along. Then they would hitch a ride back to the pool. 'Tugging', we used to call it. Dangerous it was, too. Every year, a few kids drowned. Everybody knew someone it had happened to."

*

On the Rheinfelden "Old Bridge", which connects the German and the Swiss halves of the city, there is a memorial plaque, six lines of text, for a thirteen-year-old girl who drowned in the river underneath the bridge. It is twenty Rhine kilometres upstream from Basel, the furthest you can go by ship from the sea. When you stand on the Rheinfelden bridge and look down at the river, you realise why. The bridge doesn't open, the arches are low, and an island, formerly home to a castle, juts out right where the river narrows. There, the water rages under the bridge. This turbulence is caused by the St Anna-Loch, a 32-metre-deep trench in the riverbed immediately beyond the bridge. The sudden drawdown, like a huge submerged waterfall, causes strong eddies. The water whirls, gushes, gets sucked down and churns back up. Swimmers and canoeists stand little chance here. Many have drowned.

A statue at the river's edge of a river mermaid bending lovingly over the body of a drowned girl seeks to convert the river's greedy fury into an image of youth, beauty and comfort. It was created by the sculptor Roland Kistner, from the German side of Rheinfelden, in 2007.

It was here, where the river is at its most merciless and regularly swallows up swimmers, that one spring evening, on 27 May, 2000, the thirteen-year-old Yvonne fell into the river and drowned. It was a chilly evening, ten degrees cooler than the previous day, when it had been warm and rainy. It had rained on 27 May, too—not exactly a time to be hanging about on the bridge, looking down at the river. Part of the plaque reads: *Am Rhein geboren, den Kampf mit dem Rhein hat sie verloren.* ("Born on the Rhine, she lost her battle with the Rhine.")

These lines rhyme, they embrace and repel each other. The river gives and takes lives, is the message, even those who reside on its shores and are intimately familiar with it. Just as a tiger can, in a careless moment, maul its keeper, no matter that the keeper bottle-fed it as a cub.

About a hundred people per year drown in the Rhine and its tributaries, from Switzerland to the North Sea. The river makes no distinction between men and women, children and the elderly. It devours not only the daredevils who deliberately challenge it, but also the unfortunates who find themselves in the water by accident. Regional newspapers from Graubünden to Holland report these untimely deaths all year round: tumbled, mountain bike and all, from the shoreline near Mannheim; jumped from an anchored sailboat in the Bodensee and never resurfaced; capsized in a kayak near Fuorns Medel; seized by the current from a breakwater in the Waal; sucked under by a passing ship at Uerdingen; a similar incident near Düsseldorf; pulled under in a rubber boat at the Rheinfall; or simply a five-year-old boy who went for a swim with his mother at Trebur.

The river is never blamed. At most, a sculptor chisels a mermaid to comfort the victim.

No fingers are ever pointed at the river, just as a predator cannot be blamed for being a hunter. Whenever someone drowns and reactions on social media flare up, then it's always the fault of the reckless swimmer, the lax authorities, the shortage or excess of warning signs, that inadequate fence. But never the river itself, never the tempting, often clear, always cool water that innocently flows by.

In 1530, Charles V, whose Holy Roman Empire encompassed the entire Rhine region (and more), attempted to give the river a judicial role. It was not a success. The *Constitutio Criminalis Carolina*, seen as the first body of German criminal law, took its lead from the Bamberg lawbook of 1507 and offers a chilling array of reasons for, and methods of, execution. For example, a woman who aborted her unborn baby or killed it shortly after birth was to be punished by being tied in a sack and thrown in the river to drown. That was, incidentally, only applicable, says a 1532 version, "if the comfort of sufficient water is available". Lacking that comfort, said the law, the accused was simply to be buried alive.

There was no lack of water in the Rhine and its tributaries and creeks, so until the early seventeenth century at least, on secondary rivers such as the Main, the Neckar, the Tauber and even small streams like the Franconian Rezat, platforms and ad hoc bridges were built for the purpose of hurling the offending woman – often a desperate, unwed mother – to her death.

In a city like Nuremberg, situated comfortably on the Pegnitz, infanticide cases reached the courtroom a few times a year at most, so the punishment was carried out only sporadically. The executioners didn't much care for it; they far preferred beheading, although in Nuremberg this was exclusively reserved for male offenders. Drowning was a tricky, unreliable and sometimes drawn-out business. The Romans, who also applied this punishment (for patricide), were wont to stuff a live monkey, snake, cockerel, and/or dog into the sack along with the condemned.

The women who were thrown into the Rhine and its confluents in the sixteenth century got no such company, and often had enough room to thrash about for their lives. The job of the executioner's assistant was to keep the sack submerged by prodding it underwater with a long stick. But even that didn't always work: the sack might tear, or the water was too shallow or awkwardly turbulent. It was, in short, an undignified and unnecessarily cruel operation, and one which no executioner, owing to the lack of routine, ever managed to get the hang of.

In 1580, the executioner Franz Schmidt of Nuremberg successfully lobbied to discontinue the drowning of convicted women in the Rednitz, and simply to behead them instead. On 26 January of that year, having decapitated three women for the crime of infanticide (Margaretha Doerfferlin from Ebermannsstatt, Elisabeth Ernstin from Anspach and Agnes Lengin from Amberg), he noted with satisfaction in his diary, "All three murderesses beheaded with the sword and their heads nailed high upon the scaffold. No woman ever beheaded in Nuremberg before. This was accomplished by myself and two priests, namely Meister Eucharius and Meister Lienhardt Krieg, even though the bridge for the drowning had already been erected, for they were all three to be drowned."

Margaret had left her newborn baby in the snow; Elisabeth had smashed her child's skull while in the home of a certain Herr Beheimb; and Agnes, who had delivered her baby at the home of an unnamed blacksmith, had strangled it and buried it in a rubbish heap. Two of the women were just twenty years old. There is no sign that the men who had got the women pregnant had any visitation from the law.

Franz Schmidt slept well that night. He had no issues with torturing and executing people, but the river should be left out of it.

A river is pure, it evokes associations with life, weightlessness and the passage of time; with an embrace, baptism; with origins and destinations. Everywhere along the river, from the mountain headwaters to the ocean delta, its quays, stepped banks, grassy commons and beaches are fitted out so that one can comfortably watch the water flow past.

I cannot keep my eyes off the river either, especially when it's warm out and the water is clear and cool. Where Lake Constance narrows into an easily swimmable passage from the Swiss town of Gottlieben on the south bank to the densely reedy wetlands on the German side, I sat for an endlessly pleasant hour gazing into and at the water. The pilings along the Swiss quay stand deep and distinct in the crystal-clear water. Shoals of fish are suspended in the broken sunlight. The town of Gottlieben has placed benches and swimming ladders for people like me under the shady trees along the shoreline.

Further downstream, too, I have had to hold myself back from jumping into the water. It was on the densely wooded Rhinau Island, which lies halfway between Freiburg and Strasbourg, sandwiched by the Alsace Canal and the Rhine. Inland creeks of fresh, clear water flow through the trees. I wandered around a bit, watched the reflecting sun light up the underside of the leaves, saw shoals of fish warm themselves just under the surface and noticed the water plants, clinging to a fallen tree trunk, gently sway in the clear stream.

I leaned forward, clutching onto a triangular yellow warning sign illustrating a flailing person yelling vainly for help, with the text, DANGER! RISQUE DE MONTÉE SOUDAINE DES EAUX, MÊME PAR BEAU TEMPS.*

Come on in, the water murmured, come on in.

*

I did just that, in the summer of 2019. Just north of Thusis, in Switzerland's Graubünden region, where the green water of the Hinterrhein pushes through the Viamala Gorge, I donned a tight-fitting wetsuit, helmet and water shoes, strapped a life jacket around my chest, and slid down the wet rocks to where the ice-cold water enthusiastically careers into the narrow gorge. The rocks on either side, five

* Danger! Risk of sudden high water, even in good weather

armlengths apart, rose straight up. The water was clear enough to see deep, but not all the way to the bottom.

The water levels here are regulated by the Hinterrhein hydroelectric power station which, when necessary, can release huge amounts of water at once from a reservoir upriver. When this happens, water rages through the gorge. Warning signs discourage people from descending to the river: it can happen at any moment, the signs say, even in good weather. There's an illustration of a figure running in vain from a huge wave.

I've got nothing to worry about, or so I'm told. My guide, an Englishman from the Lake District who came to Switzerland for adventure and stayed for love, has informed the hydroelectric station of our intentions, as he always does when he takes people into the gorge. He shows me a rock where I'm to sit, just above the waterfall. He explains that the water's cold. That it'll take my breath away. That I'll get used to it. That, once I've jumped in, I'll automatically bob back up, that I must let the current carry me, my feet pointed straight ahead so that, should I be thrust against a rock, my feet and legs will cushion me, that I have to keep my hands crossed against my chest, and that I mustn't resist in the rapids, just push my buttocks up so that the stones don't tear the wetsuit and injure me.

Then he looks upwards and points. "See that?"

I look. Twenty metres above us, a tree trunk spans the gorge, just under the narrow opening where the sunlight comes through. It looks like something constructed for a circus act.

"That's how high the water got last year," he says. "The river overflowed and the road to San Bernardino had to be closed."

I look up, try to picture that wall of water. The brute force. But my guide has moved on, pointing out a twisted piece of steel thicker than my arm. It looks like the work of an avalanche. "The water did that," he says. "Gives you an idea of how powerful it is, how destructive."

I look at the mangled steel. It is very convincing.

"Here we go," he says." He jumps, vanishes for a moment into the churning pool beneath the waterfall, resurfaces a bit further up.

I jump. It's exactly as he predicted.

For a good hour the river carries us downstream. Sometimes we have to swim, but mostly we just lie on our backs and look up and past the steep cliffs, where, far above us, the sun angles down through the leaves, without reaching the bottom of the gorge. The rays fracture into colours, the rocks are illuminated, water trickles and gushes and beads down. Sometimes there's a gap in the ridge, a recess where tree trunks, boulders and debris have fallen.

My guide points upwards, tells me about smuggling routes, about fugitives stealing along the gorge on their way from Italy to Switzerland. He tells me about the ocean floor, about ice ages, about various kinds of rock, each with its own character, about sediment, about gravity. The stories go downstream, I notice, just like us. It's a brotherly journey: we spin and bob side by side in the current, faces towards the light; we get to our feet together in shallow water, give each other a hand in the rapids, help each other over pebble beds, along the dripping cliffs smoothed by hundreds of thousands of years of violent water, and then back into a deep patch, the cool, soft arms of the river.

I wish it would never end. I don't want him to say that

it's over, that we have to get out, that if I went any further, I'd be a goner. That I'm already hypothermic, that I'll drown before I know it.

A river is a pure, constant and most of all compelling downward yearning.

GATEWAYS

where industry extends
to the edge of the sea
where ships spew up sand
for non-existent lots
where in the distance
a ship is piloted
into the harbour

From "Dutch landscape", Hans Wap

Near the North Sea, on the south bank of the Nieuwe Waterweg shipping canal leading to Rotterdam, is "Gateway to Europe", a snack bar housed in a Portakabin. Out front is a row of sea wind-bedraggled fan palms. Outside the cafeteria there is enough parking space for anyone wanting to sit at the wheel of their car or camper van and watch the river empty into the sea – in effect, watch life flow by.

This is the spot where just over half the Rhine's water reaches the sea. The Gateway's clientele consists mostly of Dutch people, delta dwellers who have spent their lives on land that the river has deposited. And, judging from the Gateway to Europe's busy car park, they like to watch ships come and go.

The snack-bar owner's choice of name tells me that he understood the significance of its locale: he didn't name it "Gateway to Rotterdam" or "Gateway to Holland". A moderate-sized ship entering here from the sea can push its way deep into the continent.

Contrary to what the name suggests, the Gateway to Europe's menu doesn't feature any fancy foreign stuff, but profoundly Dutch snack bar staples: frites, croquettes, frik-andel, sausages and meatballs with a wide choice of toppings.

Inside the perpetually open front door, beneath a pair of wooden clogs nailed onto the wainscot, hangs the poem

"Hollands landschap"/"Dutch landscape" by Hans Wap. Occasionally a customer will read it while their frites sizzle in the oil. Especially the last lines:

> how Dutch
> can a landscape be,
>
> one portion of frites
> one frikandel
> and two croquettes

The four motorcyclists in the queue in front of me have no time for poetry. Judging from their accent, they are Rotterdammers and they're here to eat frites and watch ships. Two men and two women, all of them over sixty. They order frites and croquettes, and don't plan to hang around at the counter. "We'll be outside," says one of them, pointing at the glass-panelled outdoor eating space. "Don't want to miss any ships. Give us a shout when it's ready."

They take up position, side by side, all four in identical shiny black-and-yellow biker suits. They look like off-duty traffic wardens. A ship carrying chemicals sails out to sea. A yacht sails in. The bow of a container ship looms around the corner of the dyke. "Maersk" says the lettering. A harmless Danish monster.

The motorcyclists do not point, and say little. Shoulder to shoulder, they gaze out into the delta. They've laid their helmets on the table in front of them. Two ships later, the frites and croquettes are ready. The blue plastic dish the frites are served in is shaped like a rowing boat.

The Northmen came out of hiding and sacked the city of Trier which, on the fifth of April, they burned to the ground, after which the citizens were either put to flight or killed. Wala, the bishop of Metz, who faced the enemy with a meagre force, was also killed.

From Liutbert, Annales Fuldenses *(Annals of Fulda)*,
Mainzer Fortsetzung, AD 882

As the youngest of three brothers, I pricked up my ears when I first heard of Charles the Fat, the last of the Carolingian dynasty. He was also the youngest of three brothers. A latecomer who watched from the sidelines as his older brothers seemed to breeze through life.

Even before he was aware of it, Charles' life was shaped by the intricate machinations of forefathers, uncles, cousins and, yes, his two older brothers. His father Louis II (known as "the German") ruled East Francia and his uncle Charles II ("the Bald") West Francia.

Those two given names, Charles and Louis, spread like weeds through the Carolingian dynasty. Every generation, every branch of the family tree, had at least one of each. They were given various, almost rustic, nicknames: the Hammer, the Great, the Pious, the Bald, the Simple, the Stammerer, the German, the Younger. These appellations were necessary because sooner or later all the Charleses and Louis either demanded a portion of the realm, or ascended or were bumped off a throne, and their descendants had to have a way of telling one from the other. With each new generation or branch of Charleses or Louis, the enormous realm that the Ur-Charles (the Great, or Charlemagne) had amassed by the sword gradually split into smaller chunks and pieces.

A monarch hoping to secure his legacy would be wise not

to bring more than one healthy heir into the world. Produce more than one son and you could count on a fight. But having only one son carried its own risk: you had to be sure he survived until adulthood, which in those days was far from guaranteed.

Charlemagne had only one legal heir, Louis the Pious, so could die happy in the knowledge that his kingdom would pass to a single monarch. But Louis' four sons – Lothair, Pepin, Charles and Louis – spent their entire lives squabbling over the succession.

Pepin died young, but Louis the Pious' death still left three brothers to tear the kingdom into separate parts. Lothair, who as the eldest son received the imperial crown, didn't manage to produce a legitimate heir, so his branch petered out after just one generation. His portion (Middle Francia, which included the Rhône, the Meuse and most of the territory west of the Rhine) was gobbled up by his remaining brothers Charles (the Bald) and Louis (the German). Louis, who got the eastern part of the empire, in turn had three sons: Carloman, Louis the Younger and Charles the Fat. These three, like a pack of hyenas, devoured bits of East Francia while their father was still alive. Charles got the short end of the stick – he was the runt, after all, and moreover suffered from epilepsy, which made it difficult for him to keep up with the other two. They thought him slow and stupid. So just half a century after Charlemagne's death, his once so massive empire had been divvied up between warring brothers, nephews and cousins.

Until they started dying. One by one, they keeled over: Carloman, who controlled Bavaria and Italy, Louis the Younger, who ruled from Alsace to Friesland. Then their uncle Charles the Bald of West Francia died, leaving an empty throne behind. Eventually, of all the legitimately born Carolingians, only the youngest brother was left. Everything that for the past decades had been divided and torn apart was swept back into one kingdom, and Charles the Fat, the young epileptic, was suddenly emperor of half the known world: the entire ungovernably vast realm of his great-grandfather.

And he, too, had no heir.

While the Carolingians were busy riling one another, the Vikings sailed into the region practically unhindered and plundered cities along the Rhine, the Meuse, the Ruhr and the Moselle. These were no swift raids, no quick retreat to sea after sacking a town. On the contrary: the Vikings felt secure enough to pitch camps where they could catch their breath after the attacks and spend the winter.

By the time Charles the Fat's last living brother Louis (the Younger) had died in 882, and Charles had returned from Rome with the papal blessing to reign over the entire East Frankish Empire, the Vikings had already extorted, pillaged and burned Zutphen, Dorestad (eight times), Xanten, Maastricht, Tongeren, Gulik, Liège, Cologne (twice), Bonn and Trier. After all this plundering, they would take their ease in riverside camps in Utrecht, Dorestad, Nijmegen, Elsloo, Duisburg and Neuss.

They didn't make it past the Middle Rhine Valley, where the river can be swift and shallow in places, so the royal residences at Mainz and Worms were spared. Not so Aachen, Charlemagne's and Louis the Pious' home base.

Charles the Fat was now emperor from Rome to Friesland, and all the rivers the Vikings rowed up fell under his rule. Likewise the wide-open Rhine delta, where heathens still sailed in from abroad. Poor, puny Charles (who, scholars currently believe, was not so fat after all) no longer had brothers to stand between him and the enemy. Now it was all down to him.

Charles had two advisers: Liutbert, bishop of Mainz and archbishop under Charles' late brother Louis, and Liutward, bishop of Vercelli and Charles' long-time chancellor. Liutbert was used to calling the shots; these Northmen, as he called them, were nothing new, and he had no illusions as to how to deal with them: force them back to sea.

But Liutward, his rival, saw things differently. He preferred baptism to banishment. Even of Northmen. Liutbert loathed him.

When Charles dismissed Liutbert and kept Liutward, the former retired to Mainz and, awaiting the fall of the last Carolingian without issue, began writing the chronicles in which he would drag the emperor and his bishop through the mud.

Emperor Charles, having travelled to Worms, conferred with his advisers, who had come from far and wide, as to how he could drive the Northmen from his empire. They took up arms and laid siege to the Northmen's fortress at Elsloo on the Meuse. Just as surrender was imminent, and the Northmen feared for their lives, one of the emperor's counsellors, one Liutward, a false bishop, bribed with money and behind the backs of the rest of the council, went to the emperor and convinced him to lift the siege.

From Liutbert, Annales Fuldenses,
Mainzer Fortsetzung, AD 882

Forgive me, Father, for I have sinned. I might be the bishop of Mainz and the archchancellor of the late Louis, who they called "the German" and who was the grandson of Charlemagne and king of all East Francia, but I can't imagine why, of all his sons, only the young Charles should survive; the runt who has achieved nothing, neither on the battlefield nor in the nuptial bed, and lends his sickly ear to that dog Liutward, the false-hearted bishop of Vercelli. Charles went to Rome and came back anointed, a puny emperor who falls to the ground at least once a day. Anyone who calls it piety should know better. His mouth was frothing at the baptismal font.

All of Louis' other sons are dead, only his bastards still slither through the palace. And our Heavenly Father has saddled Christendom not only with dead kings and castles full of living daughters and sisters, but an invasion of Northmen to boot. And with little Charles, youngest son of our former king, Louis: the baby brother who begged to be included and whose older brothers Carloman and Louis the Younger, just to be done with his whining, gave him Swabia. Have you ever been there, Father, to Swabia? But then, why would you . . . 'tis a grim backwater where the river is unnavigable, even for the heathens, and where any Christian who ventures forth ends up lost in the woods.

I know it, I have sinned, I have uttered falsehoods, or

rather, I have written them. That it was Liutward who betrayed us. And I pray for penitence, but the Heavenly Father has not yet heard my prayer.

Do you remember when word arrived that Carloman had been struck dumb and lame? He was in Italy at the time – Carloman was not only king of Bavaria, but also of Italy – and they carried him in a litter back over the mountains to his Bavarian deathbed. Before his powers of speech abandoned him, he bequeathed Italy to his younger brother. Never mind that by then he couldn't tell a hound from a hog, but no-one interceded. A month later he was dead and there was nothing more to be done. What I had been for his father, I became for young Louis, too: chancellor and confessor. As God is my witness, I keep Louis' harsh opinion of his younger brother, now emperor, locked in my heart as though in a dungeon. It was, after all, uttered in confession. Although he never repented, I forgave him time and again.

Then came the reports that the Northmen had been expelled from England and were rowing up the Rhine and the Meuse. We endured one miserable despatch after another: that Cologne burned, followed by Bonn and Maastricht and Liège. And it was precisely in those trying times that our Heavenly Father, in all his unfathomableness, also took our king Louis the Younger to his bosom, three years after his only son. The Rhineland, Alsace, our part of Lorraine, Bavaria, Saxony, Frisia – all of it was suddenly little Charles', who was then in Rome with that snake Liutward, to be anointed emperor. The whole of the Rhine, from the Alps to Friesland, from the east shore of the Meuse to the sea, was his – and wide open to the Northmen.

Up the rivers they came, like dogs scenting blood. They pitched camps on the shores, a few hours downstream from

Cologne and Maastricht, and then the plundering and slaughter started. Ships laden with booty and slaves set off for the sea. They made it as far as Trier. They killed Wala, the bishop of Metz.

Of course, we had had our share of conflicts, Carolingian family squabbles, blood feuds between brothers and cousins, but the cities had never had anything to fear. The gates stood open, the walls unguarded. But when the heathens rowed upstream to Cologne . . . just as John the Baptist preceded our Lord, so did their viciousness speed ahead, Father, like lightning before the thunder.

We were dumbstruck that they did not tow themselves along the riverbanks, but instead rowed straight up the middle. With sails hoisted. As though propelled by the devil. Why did God give them the wind at their backs? What was He trying to tell us?

The messenger who escaped saw them drop anchor at the walls of Cologne and scream at the guards. They bashed down the gate, they pissed against the walls. What they were not given, they took; what they couldn't take, they burned; anyone who resisted was killed.

They haven't made it as far as Mainz. Not yet. We must thank God, of course, but we also must fortify the walls and assemble our men. Like Charles did at Worms.

Because just then, puny Charles returned from Rome and I, grief for Louis still in my bones, had to go to Worms to bow before the runt and grin at Liutward. We had not seen each other since school at Reichenau. Have you ever met him? I was his mentor, but he took pains to contradict me. If I said north, he said south; if I wanted to fight, he chose to talk; if I spoke the truth, he wriggled around it.

How happy I was to leave Reichenau! I galloped,

buoyant with relief, to Mainz. Old Louis was still king of all East Francia; from the sea of the Northmen to the home of the bishop of Rome. He made me bishop of Mainz, later archchancellor and arch-chaplain, and I could put Liutward out of my mind.

But here he was again, a ghost from the past, right behind the throne of Louis' youngest son, in Worms. Charles had got fat – was I the only one to have noticed? He inherited nothing at all from his forebears. Have you ever heard him speak? That soft, high-pitched voice of his? He asked me about his brother's final hours. I told him that he had died peacefully, like a proper Christian, and was now in Heaven with his Maker, with the angels, and with Charlemagne.

I have always endeavoured to tell the truth, Father, as God is my witness, but even a child knows that there is a time and place for the truth. Even as I conjured up a peaceful death, it was as if my soul wavered, especially with Liutward smirking at me from behind Charles. He knew I was lying, I could tell, and with every untrue word my position weakened. Perhaps he had heard how it really went: that on his sickbed Louis begged God to make him better, and that as he lay dying, his body drenched in sweat, he saw and heard heathens everywhere, he cursed at the curtains like a coachman at an unwilling horse, and with what was left of his voice he screamed that the battlefield beckoned. And that he became calm only in his last minutes, and that in desperation I whispered in his ear, "What will become of us without you?" And that he laughed, as though God himself was laughing at me, then slipped away to the other side.

I told the emperor, "He went in peace, he did not suffer, he died piously, he was interred resplendently, and everyone is grief-stricken." He thanked me and said, "God has made me emperor of all East Francia. You were counsellor to my father and my brother, you were chancellor and confessor to them both. Our family's gratitude can never be expressed fully."

And Liutward stood there, nodding and waiting. He had folded his hands on his stomach and closed his eyes. Waiting.

Then little Charles, the chubby, epileptic weakling, relieved me of my duties, robbed me of my dignity, and thereby threw the empire to the dogs. "An emperor can have only one chancellor," he said. "My chancellor is Liutward, bishop of Vercelli. I understand you two are acquainted. He was your pupil. The empire is in good hands. Kiss each other."

. . .

Continue, my son.

That evening, Charles summoned me again. We were alone now, without Liutward. The emperor said, "I can see that your heart is dark. You have leave to return to Mainz. We shall soon do battle with the heathens. You will see us pass. You are no longer alone. I will ask you to bless my men."

"You have the blessing of Liutward, bishop of Vercelli," I said, "and of the bishop of Rome. What more can I add? I am only a servant who prays for the wisdom, health and success of my king."

I left Worms, against a stream of troops. And indeed, a month later they came to Mainz. The Lombards, Franks and Alemanni passed through the city, men on horseback, men bearing banners. Across the river were the Bavarian troops.

Liutward rode behind Charles, he was his shadow, his craven dog. They ascended the mount of the abbey of

St Alban, where I stood watching. Charles asked for the blessing, Liutward said nothing. I likewise asked him nothing. He was never planning to fight.

We looked down onto the city. The procession took hours. Charles got his blessing, but had no time, thank God, for Mass. Then they left. I did not bother to watch them go.

They marched through the Rhine Valley, past the ruins of Andernach and Bonn and Cologne, and from there through the lowlands to the Meuse, where the Northman Gotafrid had set up camp. Gotafrid knew they were coming, a quail could have heard them coming, and the attack failed. God sent hail and thunderstorms, the horses panicked and bolted into the woods, pestilence crept through the troops. Then they met at the river: the heathens inside their stronghold on the shore, our army surrounding them, the soldiers soaked and sick.

Had I been there, as councillor to my king Louis, we would have risen to the challenge, we would have been steadfast, we would have sent those heathens straight to hell. Peace would have come to the Rhineland and along the rivers. But I wasn't there, I was where I still am, here in Mainz with my parchment, and, God have mercy, my hatred.

Pray and be humble, my son.

You tell me to pray and be humble, Father, and sometimes I try to quench the fire with memories of Reichenau. You have been there, you know the Rhine is wide, the water clear, everything is bathed in sunlight, the apple trees blossom in the abbey's orchard. Then I think of the joy of my studies, the sun streaming through the round windows of the chapel, the walks along the riverbank, and discussions of the life ahead of us. But then that vision goes dark, for

Liutward is there, too. I see him arrive with the ferryman, his bag and his servant, a wealthy novice taking his first step onto the island. Most of all I see his body, the slender shoulders under his habit, the way he walked with such ease, as though nothing weighed him down. For me, everything is an effort, like wading through a pond.

Your heart is dark, my emperor said to me. Go and write. So I did as instructed and I wrote what happened with the heathens at Elsloo. Forgive me, Father, I did not write about the pestilence, the hail and the thunderstorm, but that Liutward misled the king, that it was Liutward who betrayed the men, and that the king was weak and fat and sick and sluggish and stupid, because he let himself be misled by Liutward, who had made a deal with Gotafrid. For money – of course for money, the Judas that he is.

Picture it, as I have written: the siege is coming to an end, Gotafrid and Charles approach each other, shields held high, swords lowered, the emperor of the land and the king of the sea, and Charles says to him, "Be baptised, convert to Christianity, and I shall lend you Frisia. Where the Rhine flows into the sea, the northern port of my realm, there you shall be guardians and keep your brethren from entering. I will reward you for this: with gold, with a woman from my House, women aplenty, my cousin had a daughter, Gisela, a bastard, but pretty . . ."

Shall I write that Liutward, that vile dog of a bishop, with his skinny shoulders and his skipping tread, scooped water out of the Meuse and baptised the heathen king himself? Or will no-one believe me after that?

Charles gave him two thousand pounds in gold and silver, and Gotafrid, the plunderer of our cities and our abbeys, struck camp and, loaded with Charles' gold, headed for the coast. While Charles and Liutward returned to Swabia and the people cheered as they passed, the news sped across the sea to the heathen kingdoms in the north that the emperor had given Gotafrid not only a fortune and a bride, but also authority over the river deltas. So, naturally, new ships full of heathens came swarming over the Rhineland. Robbing. Plundering. Killing.

Your heart is dark, Charles said, go and write.

I have written, Father, about the last of the Carolingians and his deceitful bishop. I have always endeavoured to tell the truth, but the truth, too, has its time and place. I now pray for penitence, for without penitence there can be no forgiveness. But God has not yet heard my prayer.

Their gill slits upward, the morgay, tope, and mudshark
approached the dykes while November
drenched and gusted, drove clouds ahead
like shoals of snook; blew goats over the rooftops

twenty hamlets splintered like gristle, white cyclone
approached from the sea

From "1421", Lowland Hymns, *Harry ter Balkt*

It's probably not accurate to say that devastating deluges always happen in the dead of night, like the North Sea flood of February 1953, but the steely darkness of a long autumn or winter night naturally lends itself to this kind of event. It bundles all manner of fears. Disaster is dark, and punishment is at its harshest when the mortals who must face it are disorientated, helpless and groggy with sleep.

I always pictured the St Elizabeth's Flood of 1421 like this: north-westerly storm, spring tide, pitch-darkness and waves smashing against the weak dykes that were supposed to protect the Groot Hollandse Waard between Dordrecht and Geertruidenberg from the threat of the sea. Villagers in Wieldrecht, Tiesselingsekerke, Almsvoet and Drimmelen either buried their heads in their straw pallets and besought Mary, or huddled together by candlelight, children on their mothers' laps, the roof beams groaning overhead. The moon – full, of course – high above the rooftops. The cattle lowed in the stalls, the odd tree toppled over. The water of the dammed-up Old Meuse, which ran straight through the polder, sloshed over its shores. The lone church bell spontaneously began tolling.

And once the water came, there was the inevitable floating cradle and loose plank with a cat, a pig, a cockerel and a milkmaid on it. This was how I imagined it.

But it wasn't spring tide, and even though the sea was

tempestuous, it was primarily water from the Merwede, which was already high because of heavy rainfall in the middle and upper reaches of the Rhine and the Meuse, and now, pushed back by the churning seawater, was looking for somewhere to spill over the dykes. The polder was already saturated and had subsided, and the dykes were poorly maintained. So when they collapsed in various places and the sea and river water surged in, there was no stopping it.

The polder was populated with villages and farms, and the fact that so many people drowned probably means it all happened very quickly. In no time, an inland sea had formed as far as the eye could see. Where church towers and tree-tops stuck out above the surface of the water. Dordrecht had become an island. Geertruidenberg was suddenly on the coast.

Above the church pews where generations of farmers and fishermen had prayed for harvests and forgiveness, shoals of bream, eel, barbel and tench now swam. Garfish lay in wait on street corners, and it wasn't long before sturgeon, shad and salmon approached from the sea over the flooded farmlands. They silently passed submerged stalls, market-places and wells on the way to their spawning grounds. As always, they swam against the current of the Rhine between the sandbanks of East and West Voorne, but where the brackish, inland sea fanned out, the route became blurred and they lost their way, searching for the river's weakened countercurrent in the inundated polder.

[. . .] In order to find the most befitting manner of determining the former course of the half Meuse along the possessions of the Prince of Orange, we all departed together on the 14th day of August from the city of St Geertruidenberg, sailing from south to north, until we passed a griend or lowland called Koosteroord which lies submerged in that drowned land, whence we sailed onwards a short distance to the north, where the Prince of Orange determined the boundaries of his possessions Standhazen, Drimmelen, Almonde, Dubbelmonde and Twintighoeven, as had been presented to us in writing [. . .]

From the proceedings determining the course of the Old Meuse through the inundated waard *of South Holland, 1560*

The agents of William, the Prince of Orange and of King Philip II of Spain did not fit into one boat, and who can say if it would have been so "befitting" if they had shared the same little barge from Geertruidenberg through the Verdronken Waard. It was meant to be a civil expedition by unbiased surveyors who would determine once and for all where, in the inundated land between Dordrecht and Geertruidenberg, the bed of the Old Meuse had once lain before land and river were erased in the St Elizabeth's Flood of 1421.

It is 1560. In another eight years, Philip and William would openly declare war on each other. But on this fourteenth of August, the 27-year-old William of Orange-Nassau had yet to rebel against the king of Spain. The current disputes are only about fishing rights in the waters of the drowned land. Philip is not only the king of Spain, but since 1555 also the Count of Holland, having been bequeathed the territory by his father Charles V, so that the fishermen to the north of the Old Meuse must pay him for fishing rights. Those who fish on the south side of the river are tenants of the Prince of Orange. Still using terms that stem from the time of Charles V, the southerners thus call themselves "fishers of the prince" and the northerners "fishers of the emperor".

But now, no-one can say with any certainty where the

Old Meuse runs, or used to, so who is to pay whom? The ownership rights of the counts of Holland and Nassau refer to the situation pre-1421, when there was still a river between the dykes of the Grote Waard. Now, however, five generations of fishermen have come and gone and the misunderstandings have piled up. The estuary's water is as murky as the mudflats, the submerged buildings that once served as boundary markers have collapsed or been dismantled. For decades, the fishers of the prince and the fishers of the emperor have resorted to fisticuffs as to who can fish where. The boundary river exists only in the minds of the leaseholders and as a drawing on an old sheet of parchment.

From Geertruidenberg, which in one tempestuous night a hundred and forty years earlier had been transformed from a rural village on the Donge to a harbour town on an inland sea, an expanse of water stretches to the north-west. The sea has pushed the river inland. The waters of the Rhine (which from the Meuse delta at Woudrichem is called the Merwede) slow down and deposit sediment. Parts of the region are becoming so shallow that they will silt up and eventually become the islands of the Biesbosch. But for now, the land is still completely under water.

On summer days it might be possible to catch a shimmering glimpse of Dordrecht from the tower of the Geertruidskerk, twenty kilometres away as the crow flies. But the towers of the submerged towns of Arnoutswaard, Dubbelmonde, Drimmelen, Erkentrudenkerc and Wieldrecht, which for years jutted above the water, have since been dismantled and the stones repurposed.

The boats have left Geertruidenberg behind and follow the submerged bed of the Donge. After a few hours' journey, the first salmon weir – a willow-branch fence nearly a hundred metres long – comes into view. The stakes and woven mesh stick out about an arm's length above the water's surface.

At the bow of the prince's barge is Adriaen Ariezoon, an elderly fisherman from Raemsdonk. Adriaen is eighty years old, the oldest fisherman on the prince's shore and still sharp enough to go along as a guide.

"Of course I know where the Old Meuse is," he says, with a fisherman's certitude. But when Arie, as a lad of ten, started fishing with his father, the St Elizabeth's Flood already dated back seventy years. So he's only guessing. The last fishermen who actually saw the river with their own eyes were old men when he was a toddler, and besides, Adriaen never much felt like listening to those old codgers' yarns; he preferred to tell them himself. So he's got no more than a vague recollection of the stories about the deluge. His grandparents were themselves infants when the north-west storm pushed the water over the dykes, the river dyke broke, and the water surged through the villages. It was the generation of his great-grandfather who, once the dead had been buried and mourned, went out to that bizarre inland sea to set up the weirs: long barriers made of woven willow branches that funnelled the salmon into a trap. No-one demanded lease money at first, so it was every fisherman for himself. After just a few years, the shallow water was teeming with shad and salmon, the surface restless with their tailfins. The weirs got longer and longer, the markets were glutted, and anarchy reigned on the water.

Only in 1516 did Charles V intervene, in an attempt to establish who owed him concession money. And the arguing began.

Adriaen points. "That weir there, that's *Doet op u ooghen*

in tijts," he says – in other words, always keep your eyes peeled. "And there," he says, pointing westward, where another one appears, "that weir belongs to the children of Adrije and Willemense. Where those weirs end to the north, that's the Old Meuse."

Every hundred metres, surveyors on both boats stick long iron staves into the water to inspect the bottom. If it's firm, then they're above former fields or meadows; if it's deeper and muddy, it's the bed of the Donge. They put down stakes. The hours pass; just as slowly, the boats proceed above the drowned river, in search of the place where it once emptied into the Old Meuse.

The fishers of the emperor, the northerners, beg to differ with Adriaen Ariezoon about the old river's course. They are sure the southerners fish far too far to the north, and that the weirs encroach into their own northern waters. The southerners, not surprisingly, are sure of the opposite. Neither group has a good word to say about the fishermen who scoop salmon out of the river downstream.

Whenever the fishers of the prince and the emperor meet on the water, at the fish markets or in the tavern, there's an inevitable tussle. The court reports and convictions speak for themselves: threats, fistfights, manslaughter. Today's expedition is meant to put an end to the wrangling.

Under the watchful eye of envoys from both parties and the witnesses Jan Ghyssen, Meeuws Hendricxz, and Cornelis Jacobsz, the surveyors – Pieter Sluyter for the Court of Holland, Cornelis Pietersz on behalf of the prince – poke their staves into the ground to determine the water's depth and take samples of the soil.

When Charles was still emperor, he tried to resolve the

controversy by simply claiming that both the north and south shores were his, and that the Prince of Orange simply had to accept it. William was still young, it was worth a try. But youngster or no, William had no intention of letting go of his fishing rights.

This is why he is here today, together with Jan VIII van Renesse, the husband of his cousin Elisabeth. They are having a jolly time on the water. A lawyer, the clerk of the general accounting office in Breda and the steward of the Oosterhout domain make sure things proceed in an orderly manner. The prince gazes out over the water, banters with old Adriaen, and raises a glass with his cousin. It is a calm, fine summer's day, ducks dart across the water, around them are the coasts of Zeeland, Brabant and Holland. And then there is the other boat alongside them, of course, with the advisers from the Court of Holland: pensioner Reynier Moons, who is mighty pleased with his status as an official from The Hague; the auditor Gerard van Rhenoy, lord of Spijk; and Joachim Hondtsocht and Arnoult Sasbouth. The craft almost sinks under their weightiness.

Once the bed of the Donge estuary has been determined (the southerners' stakes indeed stretch far too far across the Meuse; prince and cousin raise a glass to the Holland courtiers), the surveyors place a buoy and anchor it with a millstone, so that should any fishermen try to tamper with it under cover of darkness, the exact spot can be traced and the buoy replaced. And so it goes on, westwards, a meander of buoys above a river wiped off the map.

LORELEI

I know not what it signifies,
that I am so sad at heart

From Die Loreley, *Heinrich Heine*

When I boarded the ferry at Sankt Goar on the left bank of the Middle Rhine, it was early and still quiet on the river. The ferry coasted along with the current for a bit, rotated to the proper position, and steamed across the river to Sankt Goarshausen, once a village of wine, goats and salmon fishermen, but now mainly of what's left of Lorelei tourism.

From the ferry pier, a bust of Heine gazes upriver to where the nymph Lorelei looks out from the tip of a breakwater. Lorelei isn't wearing any clothes. Her front is lifelike; her back is like a hunk of melted candle wax. There is, aside from the bleating of goats on the hillside, no siren's song.

On the far shore, various footpaths lead up the cliff to the Lorelei Plateau. The path that temporarily joins the long-distance Rheinsteig hiking trail climbs steeply to Burg Katz, then proceeds at a more friendly gradient through the shady trees to the Lorelei lookout point. Just where the path levels off, there is a bench where hikers can catch their breath and look down over the cliff. There's a view of the river, both towns, the railway, passing ships. The Rhine as tiny as in a model train set. The bench being so high up, if you can tear your gaze from the scene below, you're treated to a vista over the mountains on the far side.

On that bench sat Daniela and Erhard, a retired couple from Warnemünde, a harbour town on the Baltic Sea. They slid over to make room for me to sit.

"The Lorelei was on our bucket list," said Daniela. She took off her sunglasses and looked at me with clear blue eyes. Erhard leaned round Daniela to make eye contact.

"So it's a pilgrimage," I said.

They laughed and shook their heads. Well, not exactly a pilgrimage. "We live on the Baltic Sea," Daniela told me again. "In Warnemünde."

"But the Lorelei is still a must-see," I said. "Even if you grew up in the East."

They both nodded.

"We lived in the GDR for most of our lives," Daniela said. I realised that for her, the border was subconsciously still there somewhere.

Back in 1986 I bought the complete works of Heine in a shop in East Berlin. Five volumes, Aufbau Verlag, gold on blue, seventeenth edition, with a preface by the former World War II resistance activist and East German *Kulturpolitiker* Helmut Holtzhauer. His introduction begins with the observation that Heine not only knew Marx and Engels, but that he witnessed the revolutions of his time and the foreshadowing of the inevitable collapse of civic society.

"Did you have to memorise *Die Loreley* at school?"

"No," Erhard said. He thought for a moment and added, "But you could if you wanted to."

"But you couldn't visit it," I said.

For a moment no-one spoke. We just gazed down at the river.

"Heine was a tormented man," Erhard said to break the silence. "And a bit of a victim."

"But here we are," said Daniela. She looked over her shoulder at the path that climbed further up the hill. "Almost." She turned back and pointed at the mountains across the river. "You can see for miles here. I like that. The horizon."

We all watched as the clouds in the west moved slowly northwards over the Hunsrück mountains.

"What's the difference, do you think, between people who live on a river and those who live on the sea?" I asked.

"For me, a river is dynamic. It's a route, a link," Daniela said. "People are always busy, something is always passing by."

"People who live on the sea are more laid back," Erhard agreed.

"The sea has a far side, too," I said. "It's just further away."

"There was a ferry that went from Warnemünde to Denmark," Erhard said. "Once, a guy hooked his boat to the ferry and hitched a ride to the West. Then the border patrol built watchtowers, so you couldn't do that anymore."

"Yes," Daniela said. "They took good care of us."

We laughed.

"The idea was good," she said. "It was the people who were bad."

"So why didn't you come straight to the Lorelei when the Wall fell?" I asked. "Seems like it wasn't so high on your bucket list after all."

"We lived on the Baltic coast," Daniela said, yet again. "When the Wall fell, we jumped into our Wartburg – we had a Wartburg – and drove straight to the North Sea. You know why?"

She looked at me expectantly, laughter lines radiating from her blue eyes.

"Tell me," I said.

"The Baltic doesn't have tides. This was something we wanted to see with our own eyes. So we drove to the nearest North Sea coast and stood there for a long time, staring out at the sea. And sure enough, the water came in and went out just like they said. We hadn't any money to stay overnight, so we slept in the car. When we'd seen enough, we drove back home."

Up on the Lorelei cliff is a landscaped observation park. There's a summer toboggan run and an open-air theatre, and pillars throughout the park which, for a euro, will recite a poem. From the visitors' centre it's a straight walk to the lookout, a hundred and thirty metres above the Rhine, where enormous German flags flap on their masts.

Having left the bench before Erhard and Daniela, I passed them again on my way down from the lookout. I watched as they continued side by side up the hill, unhurriedly, getting smaller and smaller beneath all those flapping flags.

*

It rained last night, but now that the sun is peeking out above the Lorelei rock it's warming up. The moisture is evaporating from the asphalt on the road this side of the Rhine; across the river, a train traces a trail of sparks along the overhead wires. Back on my side, a car slows and turns into a car park from where you can walk out to the statue at the end of the breakwater. An older couple (age: first grandchild is walking, the second is on the way) get out. His drooping shoulders and sagging belly betray a sedentary existence, but she is slender and armoured in the typically German elegance of a tailored trouser suit and meticulously disciplined, mid-length blonde hair.

This look took more than a hairbrush.

A path runs along the spine of the breakwater, which stretches for half a kilometre parallel to the shore. At the very end, the statue of the Lorelei looks out at the passing ships. The woman says something to the man, who unlocks the just-locked car and takes out a camera. While he's busy adjusting the cord so it hangs on his belly, she's already walked off. They pass a sign saying UNEBENER FUSSWEG ZUR LORELEYSTATUE. BETRETEN AUF EIGENE GEFAHR. They've been warned: the footpath is uneven, use it at your own risk. She steps over the rocks as though over loose ice floes. There is a smile on her lips.

The path is long, the man is at pains not to stumble or twist his ankle, but she seems to float. Occasionally he stops and looks upstream through the trees, reaches for his camera, but seeing his wife in the distance he hurries on after her, then stops anyway to take a picture. It takes them a good twenty minutes to reach the tip of the breakwater, at the nymph Lorelei. The woman glances up at the bronze statue looking out over the Rhine. Then she turns to the river and inspects the gravel below, which lies fanned out at the end of the dam as though draped there, like a veil. The water sploshes impatiently.

A few sloping concrete slabs offer the visitor the opportunity to go down to the water's edge. The woman susses out the situation, judges the angle from which her husband must photograph her, positions herself at the foot of the statue and starts issuing him with directions. He listens carefully, tries to understand, follows her instruction to make his way down the concrete slabs, and once there turns and lifts the camera to his face.

"Back up," she commands. He lowers the camera and looks up at her. "Further back," she says, flapping her hand. He glances behind him and takes a few steps back. Again positions her in the viewfinder.

"Further," she says.

He takes another step back, keeping his eye on her through the lens. She tries out a pose, then another, inhales, looks out over the river, lifts her chin slightly. She attempts, and finds, the pose of a goddess; she knows what she's doing. The man points his camera, lowers it, fixes some setting or other, brings it back to his face.

Then she waves her hand again, without looking at him.

"Further," she says. "Further . . ."

The man turns and looks, but one more step means landing in the river. The water is not deep. He takes that step.

Does he love his wife? Does he fear her?

He points the camera, takes the photo.

The woman directs her gaze over his head, at the barge *Camaro II* that's just going past. She's transporting not only dozens of sea containers piled high, but also, strapped to her side, a dismantled lightship, strayed far from the sea. On her wheelhouse, in big white block letters, is the name SOUTH ROCK. The *Camaro II* puffs by, unperturbed; her wake is heading for the man, who is still standing in the water, but he has lowered the camera and is asking his wife something.

She does not answer. She is humming, she is a nymph. He looks up at her, breathless. When the *Camaro II*'s wake reaches him and the water sloshes into his shoes, he shudders slightly, but does not step onto dry land.

BASEL

The river is a man. If you jump in,
it takes you in its arms and cradles you.

Katja Reichenstein, founder and owner of the
Gannet, a restaurant/cultural centre in Basel

The lightship being pushed up the Middle Rhine valley is called the *Gannet*. She had served for fifty-five years at South Rock in the Irish Sea, two miles off the coast of County Down. South Rock, a low stony outcrop, is a hazard to mariners, disappearing entirely during spring tides. It is identifiable only by the breakers washing over it. At the rock's highest point is a now-disused lighthouse. It was replaced in the nineteenth century by the lightship *Gannet*, with her beacon amidships, anchored just to the west of the Rock. Until the summer of 2009. Then the *Gannet* was decommissioned and towed to shore.

She was Ireland's last lightship. Where the *Gannet* and her nine-man crew were once anchored (54° 24′ N, 5° 21′ W), a buoy now bobs. The *Gannet*'s job, in those narrow waters between Ireland and Scotland, was to warn and reassure ships travelling to and from Belfast. Once, she was blown off anchor and had to be towed back to her rightful coordinates. Otherwise, she withstood the storms that tossed her and survived the fogbanks that made her invisible to passing ships. Then she would blare her foghorn every few minutes.

All this was behind her when she was en route to her final destination, a quay in Basel, just over Switzerland's borders with Germany and France where the Rhine's waters leave the country. There, she would be hoisted onto dry land, a foreign body hurled by an imaginary tsunami into the midst of a makeshift commune of alternative cafés on the Uferstrasse.

That she got there at all is thanks to the efforts of Tom Brunner and Katja Reichenstein, a Swiss couple who discovered the *Gannet* at Port Werburgh, an English tidal harbour on the north shore of the Medway, near Chatham in Kent. At low tide, the *Gannet* lay dry in the mud, at high tide she bobbed among other down-at-heel boats. Two more decommissioned lightships were moored along the harbour's outer quay.

The then-owner of the *Gannet*, a Frenchman, had transported her to the east of England. His idea was to take her to Paris, just across the Channel. But his plan fell through and there she lay, rusting in the mud. An inglorious end to an exhilarating life of service. Until Tom Brunner and Katja Reichenstein spotted her.

What possessed the Swiss couple to travel to England, climb aboard the *Gannet* and do a tour of the officers' cabins, the crewmates' bunks, the windowless wheelhouse, the engine room, the helicopter deck and the light mast? And above all, what was it that made them buy the ship and transport her all the way along the Rhine?

"Homesickness," Katja says as we talk in the shipyard at 's Gravendeel. The *Gannet* had just been towed across the North Sea and up the Haringvliet and the Dordtsche Kil to be dismantled.

"Or wanderlust," says Tom.

We stand on the quay and watch as the welders take their torches to the foghorn, which sticks up from the deck like a pillar, to dislodge it from its base.

"What do you mean, homesickness, wanderlust?" I ask.

"We live in Basel," Katja says, "so for us, the Rhine is a lifeline. Not only a gateway to abroad, but also a harbinger of the sea. And when all you've got are mountains, you yearn for the sea. The sea means holidays, the sea means freedom, the sea simply means a break from Switzerland."

Tom nods. "I've pissed in the Rhine a lot," he says. "And every time, I think: that's going to end up in the sea." He nods over his shoulder towards the west and puts a cigarette between his lips.

We're quiet for a moment, allowing Tom's image to sink in, and look at the light mast, still standing proudly some eleven metres above the quiet water of the harbour.

"A river comes from somewhere and goes somewhere," Katja says. "And whenever I stand at the Rhine, I think: this is going to the sea."

"If you stand at the Rhine, which way do you look?" I ask. "Upstream or downstream?"

"Always downstream," Tom and Katja answer in unison.

Katja Reichenstein was born in Basel in 1973. Her father had a barber shop and her mother worked as a paediatric nurse at the local hospital. Both parents had lived on the Rhine all their lives: father in Basel, mother in Stein am Rhein further upstream where, under the Rheinbrücke, the clear green water of the westernmost branch of the Lower Lake Constance suddenly picks up speed and begins its restless journey to the sea. From there, the river water gurgles between the wooded shorelines – Switzerland on the south bank, Germany on the north. Just outside Schaffhausen it crashes violently over Europe's most powerful waterfall, the Rhine Falls; at Leibstadt it cools a nuclear reactor; under the Rheinfelden Bridge it lures tragic souls into its whirlpools; only when it arrives in Basel does the river slow its pace. It becomes a bit more relaxed, a bit more stately, as though all those sophisticated eyes are on it and it has to mind its manners. The Baslers saunter along the promenade or sit on the steps leading down to the water's edge to watch it flow past, or to admire the reflection of the sunlight, or just to pass the time.

Whether you live on the high bank, with the cathedral, the government offices and the ornate city hall, or on the less well-off lower bank, where everyday folk and day-trippers stroll: every citizen of Basel feels a connection to the river, which brings light to the city and provides room for the wind.

On Sundays, the Reichensteins would stroll under the trees and along the outdoor cafés of the Untere Rheinweg, on the city's lower bank. Sometimes they would take the cable ferry across the river and Katja would watch the water splosh under the boat.

That water comes from the mountains, she learned, but flows out to sea. On the other side of the old bridge, around the bend, over there – that's another country. That is where the long journey north begins.

In the summer she would watch as townspeople jumped from the bank, their clothes bundled in a waterproof, floating Wickelfisch bag, and let the current carry them downstream, under both bridges.

"The river is a man," Katja says a year later when I visit her in Basel, and we watch the water flow by. "Always in a hurry, always restless. The river is strong, it's a macho guy."

"And here's me thinking it was a woman," I say.

"A lake is more womanly," Katja says. "The river is a man. If you jump in, it takes you in its arms and cradles you."

I tell her I'm surprised to see how Swiss people can't resist stripping off their clothes and jumping into a river. Not only in Basel; I'd seen it in Bern, too: whooping Swiss being carried along by the Aare.

"Must be a Swiss thing," I say. "We Dutch wouldn't do it, at least not where the current is strong."

"Really?" she says, genuinely surprised. "Then what *do* you people do with the river?"

Tom Brunner, born just outside Bonn, is the son of a garage owner. While his father was repairing cars, Tom would slice open the back seat, install speakers, and neatly stitch up the upholstery. He turned cars into mobile discotheques. Now he's turning a lightship into a music venue.

"Since he's not from here and isn't burdened by local sensitivities, he comes up with ideas that would never occur to me," Katja says. "He came to Basel, saw the art museum's courtyard, and thought: what a cool place to do live radio broadcasts. For a native Basler, this would be out of the question, as if it's sacred ground. Tom doesn't have any of that baggage, so he gets all kinds of stuff done. He broadcast from that courtyard for five summers. That's how we met."

Katja leads me across the long plank onto the lightship. The *Gannet* is on dry ground, like Noah's Ark. She's got a shiny new coat of paint, the metal's been scraped clean of rust, and the light mast, which had been removed back in 's Gravendeel so the ship could pass under the Rhine bridges, once again towers above the rest. At night, its beam swoops over the Rhine.

On deck, two construction workers are putting away their tools. Their workday is finished, and from the upper deck you can see the bars and restaurants along the quay filling up with young Basler. They come to this urban fringe by bike or on foot, all of them spurred by the need to shake off the rigid, orderly Swiss way of life. The city's housing blocks look down upon this colourful anarchy from a distance. Somewhere in those flats are angry residents who regularly call the police to complain that they can't sleep because of the racket, and that those radical lefties on the quay must be got rid of!

Katja leads the way to where the restaurant will be. Now that everything's been ripped out, the ship looks bigger on the inside than I remember her. Via cast-iron spiral stairs reclaimed from Brixton tube station, we descend below deck to where a stage has been constructed. Here, too, all the interior bulkheads have been removed. Where the generators for the windlass and light mast once hummed and the sailors slept is now a space that will host some three hundred concertgoers.

Later, sitting at one of the cafés and looking over at the *Gannet* towering above all the rest, the conversation turns to the 's Gravendeel shipyard, to the workmen who had to remove as much surplus weight as possible so the lightship would not run aground in the shallow parts of the Rhine.

"Just thirty centimetres to spare," Katja says.

We talk about how Ad Dubbelman, the owner of the *Camaro II*, was happy to lash this unusual cargo to the side of his barge with steel cables, and how he said that the window of opportunity was small – a matter of a few days – for the barge to pass over the shallow stretches between Lorch and Trechtingshausen. And how, when they arrived, all of Basel came to watch the enormous crane hoist the *Gannet* out of the river, how she slowly floated from water to quay, the dripping ship, almost six hundred tons of steel, the heaviest object ever lifted in Switzerland. She fitted neatly into the cavity that had been dug for her.

All at once, there were no more angry residents and no more radical lefties. They were all Baslers, looking up with tears in their eyes at that 600-ton yearning from the north that had hopscotched from sea to harbour to ship-yard to land. She had made her way upstream to their city, against the current, like an offering, a reassurance, a portent, a connection, a beacon.

Katja rubs her arms. It's a warm summer's evening, but she feels a sudden chill.

"One of the first things we did when she was on the quay was to reattach the light mast, so she was a proper lightship again. And we turned on the light. You know what happened then? A storm. A tempest. No sooner had the ship been put into place, the wind started blowing like crazy. Really strange, because that hardly ever happens here. It was so violent that trees were uprooted, roof tiles blew off and the power went out. The city was completely dark, it was really frightening. And in that darkness, one single light shone: the beam from the ship's light mast. She stood there, sweeping her light over the city, like a beacon of calm in the storm."

Katja falls silent, Tom lays a reassuring hand on hers, and I look over at the *Gannet*: a wayward sea monster washed ashore.

WORK AND PRAYER

There are gods living in the Rhine. Not only Rhenus Pater – whom the Romans portrayed as Neptune, with bushy beard and a pair of horns, as though he's bearing the two prongs of the delta, and who swam up the river from the sea – but also countless other gods, older than Rhenus, whose names we don't know or who've been forgotten. They dwell not only in the main river, but in all the tributaries, lakes, streams and swamps in the Rhine's path, everywhere where there's water.

They may have withdrawn from the world, but their household effects, money and weaponry still surface during dredging operations or in the summer, when the water is at its lowest.

You can imagine that, before the time of the Romans and their written language and when life was still predictable and infinite, the gods were less timid and could be seen every now and then. By a farmer, for instance, walking along a forest path, hidden by the trees from the god's eye, catching sight of a water nymph or a deity through the branches, sunning themselves on the bank of a creek like a cold-blooded creature, their wet hair drying in the sun. One unforgettable glimpse, a ripple in the water, and it was gone.

Perhaps it was out of fear (or, who knows, pity) that mortals offered the gods gifts. This happened not only in the known locales, like Neuchâtel, where a modern-day construction project uncovered a Celtic weapons trove, but also in every nook and cranny of the river basin, as I learned from archaeologist Henny Groenendijk. I met him just outside the Groningen town of Smeerling, about ten kilometres from the Dutch–German border. Smeerling is situated in an adjacent tiny river basin, where the Ruiten Aa wriggles its way north to the Westwoldse Aa and empties into the Dollard Bay.

Henny brought me to the spot where he dug up an urn field in the 1980s, where the Iron Age Westwolders buried their cremated dead. The ash-filled urns were taken to the Galbargen, today no more than a gentle rise to the side of some fields along a provincial road, but in its day it was a prominent hillock rising above the fenland.

"I found the grave of a very young child," he said. "Great care had been taken with the burial. The infant had been given a small pot, maybe with food for its journey. Later, as if to make room for the parents, the grave was expanded. They dug a keyhole-shaped ditch, almost a moat, all around it, and then built a mound inside it."

"If we'd been there then, what would we have seen?"

"Just people like you and me, dressed in woollen clothes; farmhouses you could picture being liveable: vertical supports, wattle and daub walls, one space for livestock and one as living quarters. Really not much different from what you might have encountered a hundred years ago."

I tried to envisage them approaching the Galbargen; the whole settlement, twenty-five people, beards, braids, their clothes a dull brown, grey, dirty white. Someone carried the tiny urn. I scoured my imagination, searched amongst the mourners.

"Was there a priest?"

Henny shrugs. "I don't know. Maybe. They had their rituals, of course. They also left offerings, preferably in wet places: swamps, creek beds. No-one knows exactly why."

Catuvolcus, king of half of the Eburones, had united
with Ambiorix, king of the other half, in the insurrection
against the Romans, but was now an old man and could
not contemplate war or exile. He cursed and denounced
Ambiorix for choosing to rebel. He then killed himself
by eating of the yew tree, which grows very commonly
in Gaul and Germany.

From The Gallic War, *Julius Caesar*

They say that Ambiorix swam across the Rhine as he fled from the Romans, but that our king Catuvolcus was too old and feeble to take flight, so drank the sap of the sacred yew tree in order to join the gods. And that it took him a long time to die. For years he hadn't been able to eat properly, and he probably trembled all the more from the stress as he drank the poison. They say he slid from his stool and, lying on the ground, begged the gods for death. His wives left him to his fate. They heard the Romans approach and fled into the woods. The men had long since deserted or had been killed. But Catuvolcus was too old and too slow, but mostly too exhausted, to run from the Romans. Ambiorix, of course, was long gone.

This is how the Romans must have found Catuvolcus: abandoned and crumpled on the ground next to his cauldron.

He had visited our village to offer a sword to the Rhine. I was still a child. The first rumours of a legion of invaders were already making their way upriver: that a large army from the south had defeated Ariovistus. And that this army was heading our way. We had no idea how strong they really were.

I can still see him entering our village, Catuvolcus on his horse. His whiskers were already white, but he dismounted without assistance. He had Ambiorix with him, introduced him to the men as their new leader. Ambiorix began speaking. If he had told us that the river flowed towards the sunrise, or that horses laid eggs, we'd have believed him. Even the sheep listened. They should hang him from that torque around his neck.

He had sweet-talked Catuvolcus as well. They would share the regency. But a throne is not easily shared – just ask the gods. You could tell that Catuvolcus was losing his grip. He called his men together, us too, everyone. He gave the village elder a handful of coins, tried to explain, could not find the words. Ambiorix took over from him.

No-one had ever seen a coin, no-one understood what it was for. Even Catuvolcus had no idea. Tiny golden saucers, scarcely bigger than the tip of your little finger. Ambiorix was holding forth: every little saucer was called a *stater*, he said. That was the name of the coin, a sacred sign of camaraderie, like a glass armband or a torque, or a shield or sword, only more valuable. Whoever shared the coins would band together. Against the intruders from the south. They also had coins, just different ones. It was he who called them Romans. New words – always new words whenever Ambiorix spoke.

And Catuvolcus just sat there staring at those coins in his hands. The sun made them sparkle, speckled his face with light. He mumbled something, but no-one paid him any attention. They were focused on Ambiorix and his magic words. I stood near the old king, took a step closer.

"I can't make out what's on them," I heard him mutter with his foresty accent. "A horse . . .? No, no . . ." He looked up, saw me, smiled, shook his head.

When Ambiorix had finished, and the men cheered and everyone started promising and swearing things left and right, Catuvolcus raised his arms and everyone fell silent.

"Take us to the river."

The water was shallow enough for the horses, the bank was dry, the priests led the way, they sang, they blew the carnyx, the men followed, we all followed, and we sang and beat drums as though we were going off to fight the enemy.

One of Catuvolcus' men brought him a piece of cloth. He took it, underneath it was a sword. It glimmered, it was brand new. He held it out in front of him with both hands, like a newborn, a girl, a young animal, an offering.

When they reached the river, the place where the whirlpools are, where the gods pull the human children down into the depths, the priests, Catuvolcus, Ambiorix and our headman went up onto the platform.

The carnyx ceased, the priest sang, Catuvolcus raised the sword above his head; for a moment all was quiet, the priest raised his eyes, we all raised our eyes, and when the crows flew overhead, Catuvolcus dropped the sword into the water. The headman threw the coins in after it. Then the others followed. A shower of coins.

Then the drums and the carnyx burst forth again. The men shouted, ducks flew off in fright.

This was years ago. The gods did not want to help us. It's said that Ambiorix misled the Romans, lured them into a trap. By the time they realised their mistake, it was too late. Then their leader came with his army and slew nearly everyone.

A few of us escaped, we went downriver to the islands, surrendered to the mercy of the men there. We watched our village burn as we sailed away. Romans pissed off the platform into the river.

The Eburones are no more.

. . . there the droplet, trickled from the chalice,
colours the ocean . . .

From "Οἴνου ἑνα σταλαγμόν"
("Of wine a drop"), J.H. Leopold

There is a basilica in the town of Echternach, Luxembourg, a Romanesque church with a sober apse, where a long, straight staircase leads down to the crypt. There, behind a metal grille, with candles burning on either side, is the marble sarcophagus of Saint Willibrord, Apostle to the Frisians. The casket is enclosed in a miniature Gothic church made of heavenly white stone, lit from within and overgrown with sculpted angels and watchful dog-headed dragons, and supported by stumpy marble pillars which in turn rest upon the backs of patient lions. It gives the impression of standing a tiny bit crooked, as though when it was put in place, the workmen had a difficult job balancing the heavy ensemble, and the suggestion to shift a few things before lunch was roundly vetoed. And that the workmen fled the chilly crypt, returning to the land of the living, to a meal of *Judd mat Gaardebounen* (pork collar with broad beans) or *Feiersténgszalot*, a traditional meat salad. Their footsteps and voices faded away, leaving Willibrord alone in his crooked casket.

And yet it did not go entirely quiet in the crypt. From deeper in the ground came a drip-drip-drip, with short intervals, into shallow water. It was a hollow, echoing, but also surprised sound, as if they were not water drops but falling question marks. They echoed as though in a spacious cavern. Willibrord, a man of rock-solid convictions, will have to endure until Judgment Day the ordeal of a never-ending litany of questions from underneath his resting place.

The candles around the sarcophagus flicker faintly. A draught wafts up from the pitch-black corner of the crypt whence the sound of dripping comes. Because there, a staircase chiselled out of rock descends yet deeper underground. Even armed with a candelabrum or torch, it takes courage to go down into the Stygian gloom, towards the dripping. Shadows dance against the walls, the echo of the drops soon drowns out your footsteps.

But the descent does not take long. After twenty irregular steps, the floor levels off into a small room with a stone basin. Water sweats out of the wall, collects in a shell carved out of stone, and then drips into the basin before disappearing through a drain.

On the wall is a fresco of a beardless saint, still a youth, his right hand raised and his left hand holding a staff. The look in his eyes is that of a schoolboy who's just been slapped, has shed a few tears, and is now minding his Ps and Qs. Above his head is the text, *Haurietis aquas in gaudio de fontibus salvatoris*, from the Book of Isaiah, 12:3: *With joy you shall draw water from the wells of salvation*. That the youthful saint doesn't look at all joyous probably has to do with the text which precedes the quote: *I will praise you, Lord, though you were angry with me*.

Alcuin of York was just a toddler when Willibrord was interred at Echternach; he never met the man in real life. But half a century later, by then a scholar in Aachen and author of *The Life of Willibrord*, he would recall with conviction how Willibrord, the son of converted heathens from Northumbria, began a religious life in York, endured the rigours of the abbey of Rath Melsigi, Ireland, and in the autumn of 690, encouraged by his tutor Egbert, crossed the North Sea to convert the Frisians. He and a handful of fellow monks landed, wrote Alcuin, in the Rhine delta and stopped there for refreshments before travelling further. He used this break to confer with his brothers on how to proceed.

At issue was whether to travel directly to Utrecht or to first drop in on the Frankish king Pepin. But Utrecht, they learned, was still firmly under the control of the Frisian warlord Redbad, so they decided to give Utrecht a miss.

Redbad had little patience with newcomers haranguing his fellow tribesmen with incomprehensible stories of sin, guilt, afterlife, eternal damnation and forgiveness.

The fate of the missionaries Ewald and Ewald, whose dismembered bodies were found drifting in the Rhine, underscored the wisdom of Willibrord's decision to give the land of Odin a wide berth. The two Ewalds, born far to the north, on the Baltic Sea, had at a young age sailed away from their tribe. Their contemporary, the historian the Venerable Bede, wrote, "They were both equally devout and even shared the same name, for they were both called Ewald, but with this difference: owing to the colour of their hair, the one was called Black Ewald and the other, White Ewald."

Black Ewald was the more learned of the pair; White Ewald's job was mainly to carry the sacred altar plank and the sloshing casks of holy water. This is how they returned to the continent: pale-eyed eccentrics who would alternate between muttered prayers and full-throated song. They wisely avoided sailing to their own village on the Baltic Sea, where they probably dared not show their faces, but rather up the Rhine, past the land of the Frisians, until villages appeared on the shores where Saxons lived and spoke the language they, the Ewalds, had learned in England and Ireland. There they disembarked. Black Ewald did the talking, White Ewald followed with the holy attributes. The village elder offered them lodgings in his house, where they, at Black Ewald's request, would await a meeting with the headman.

"I have a gift for him," Ewald said.

Conversations on a riverbank generally follow an expected tack. The question of where you come from is obvious from the moment you come sailing in: either upstream or downstream. Upstream were the Franks, and beyond them the Alemanni; downstream were the Frisians, and beyond them, the sea.

Your business there is also fairly straightforward: you've come either to bring something or to take something. The trouble started with what exactly these men brought, and what they hoped to take with them. "We come with a great gift," Black Ewald repeated. "A treasure, in fact, for the salvation of the soul and for eternal life, deliverance from all one's sins." He began to sing.

Then the village elder began to suspect that something was up. Salvation of the soul, release from sin: strange notions indeed. A treasure? Maybe. There might be something of value in those casks. He gave the Ewalds food, as one does with strangers, left the hut and conferred.

The next day, his scepticism was confirmed. The two guests kept on singing and praying and churning out gibberish. The headman was on his way, but who *was* he, anyway? A chosen leader, some harmless dimwit, a counsellor at best, who in the end had to answer to freemen like the village elder. Here at the river it was he, the elder, who ran the show and oversaw the temple to which offerings were brought. The headman still hadn't arrived, so the village elder was free to act as he saw fit.

His hunch that his guests were Christians, like those who lived far upstream amongst the Franks and the Alemanni, and that they might win over the headman, caused him some concern. A scenario that upset the established order of things, that forced him – the village elder, a free man! – to partake of a rite whose hero was a dud, to witness the dismantling of his temple, income and all, and to suddenly have to worry about something as incomprehensible as saving his own soul – this made him at first uneasy, then furious, then resolute. He summoned his guests to an open spot along the river, led them into a circle of men and demanded to know their true intentions.

White Ewald glanced around nervously. Black Ewald, the spokesman, asked, "Is the headman nearly here?"

"The headman is on his way," the village elder said. "Go ahead and begin."

"Shall I fetch the plank and the holy water?" asked White Ewald, pointing to the house of the elder.

"Plenty of water here," said the elder, with a nod towards the river.

"The water we bring is blessed and holy," said Black Ewald.

"Where does that water come from?"

"From above."

"Rainwater, you mean," said the elder. Laughter.

"The water we bring was taken from the river, but has been consecrated by a servant of God," Black Ewald said, now raising his voice somewhat. "And on the Day of the Lord's resurrection, it will wash away your sins, as it has done with us, provided you swear devotion to the Almighty God, and turn your back on the devil. Then this water, after the day of your death, will bring you eternal life in bliss and in the presence of the eternal, God the Father of Jesus the Christ, who—"

"Do you see that temple, there?" the elder interrupted. "I notice you have not yet done your sacred duty. No offerings, nothing. If you have a gift, then offer it at the temple; not after death, but now. The gods are all around us, we are free men who do as the gods bid us, and for the rest as we please."

If Black Ewald had just held his tongue, his fate might have been the same as White Ewald's. But no. They killed White Ewald swiftly with a sword, Bede writes, but Black Ewald suffered prolonged torture and his limbs were ripped in a gruesome manner from his body, after which both corpses were thrown into the Rhine.

This was clearly not the way to go about it, even though Willibrord's objective was the same as that of the two Ewalds: to convert and baptise the heathens with the very water in which they sailed, fished and pissed; which they drank and where they watered their livestock; with which they cooked and bathed; where they swam and offered swords; and where a god occasionally tarried.

But Willibrord was more prudent than the missionaries who, holy water in one hand and a sacred plank in the other, traipsed through the pagan land above the Rhine, singing psalms all the way.

So as soon as he reached the coast he dropped anchor, went ashore and after conferring with his companions, suggested they take a detour via Pepin, the Frankish ruler who had not only the right faith, but the right armies.

Whichever river mouth they moored at, the detailed and meticulous tale that followed – of seafarers surviving a stormy autumn crossing, going ashore and, the sea still in their legs, taking some refreshment before carrying on – suggests an eyewitness account. And it could well be, for Alcuin based his biography on the unpolished writings of a contemporary of Willibrord, a Scot or Irishman who may have been present then and who later mainly recalled that, high on those dunes, after all those fearful moments in the wild surf, he clutched a flask of wine to his breast as though it was his lover.

Willibrord waited until Pepin had defeated Redbad and the region was safe to travel through. Top-down Christianity: the son of a heathen as an instrument in the hands of a Frankish monarch. An emissary of the pope, no less, whom he'd twice visited at Pepin's insistence, so that he could do his holy work under the title Archbishop of the Frisians. Without too much danger to his own person, Willibrord travelled the territory around the river mouth in order to consolidate the power of the Franks in the delta and, with it, their access to the Rhine.

He built many churches, one where the cathedral of Utrecht now stands. And he founded a monastery in Echternach. Amongst the miracles he performed (as reported by Alcuin, presumably retelling the account of the thirsty Celtic seafarer) are numerous instances of jars of wine that never ran dry, no matter how much was poured from them.

After Pepin's death, Willibrord was forced to abandon Utrecht, where he had settled. He and his fellow monks fled from Redbad, who recaptured the territory, destroyed Willibrord's churches, and sailed up the Rhine to Cologne with his men. Willibrord did not depart this world chopped up in the river like the poor Ewalds, but – entirely in his own style – peacefully at eighty-one in bed in Echternach, where he was interred in a slightly too short sarcophagus in the catacombs of his abbey church, and whence to this day the consecrated droplets, homeopathically diluted, flow from the local river Sûre along the Moselle to the Rhine, and from there spread throughout the pagan lands to the north, until they disperse in the ocean.

For what has man for all his labour [. . .]
with which he has toiled under the sun?
All the streams run to the sea,
and yet the sea is never filled.

Ecclesiastes

In Besigheim, just before the Enz feeds into the Neckar, barriers have been constructed in the river to maintain the water level and boost the flow. After heavy rainfall, the water plunges into a side stream, and via this detour it reaches the Neckar. The controlled main current continues to flow calmly between the straightened banks to a small hydroelectric plant built in 1901 by Wilhelm Röcker, a manufacturer of nails and hobnails. By the end of the nineteenth century, Röcker had seen a rise in demand for his product and cranked up production to the point where the traction engine that powered his factory could no longer keep pace, and broke down.

Not long thereafter, his factory burned to the ground. Röcker looked on the bright side, concluding it was a blessing in disguise.

So, in 1901, with an entrepreneur's thirst for expansion, he rebuilt the factory, bigger and better, and purchased the old Besigheim watermill, which he then tore down and replaced with a hydroelectric power station. The functionally designed station spanned the Enz, and its three turbines produced enough electricity not only for Röcker's nail factory, but for all of Besigheim.

In a sense, he was just following in the footsteps of his father Ernst Conrad Röcker, who, barely half a century earlier, had siphoned off water from the Steinbach, a small tributary of the Enz with an unpredictable flow rate, to power a machine that produced hobnails. But all this was before German unification, before industrialisation, when things happened on a small scale and if there wasn't enough rain, the machine simply ground to a halt and no hobnails were made until the current picked up again.

Wilhelm Röcker (not for nothing a namesake of the Kaiser) wrenched the company out of this hit-or-miss operation and into industrialised Germany, where construction was booming and nails were in high demand. He soon had a hundred employees working in shifts, churning out nails with machines driven by power harnessed from the Enz.

Like all things, this too came to an end. Two world wars had swept Röcker's nail production to unheard-of heights, but peacetime ushered in a downward spiral. When builders said farewell to the nail in favour of the screw, Wilhelm's successor threw in the towel. Over nearly a century, the Röckers had manufactured more than 4,500 different kinds of construction nail, but not one of them could rescue the business. And demand for hobnails had long ceased. It was 1974.

Out for an after-dinner stroll along the Enz one day in May, I was struck by how drowsy and tranquil the river was. Swallows darted over the surface, wagtails hopped about under the flowering irises on the shore, and in the alder and maple trees, thrushes vied in song. From the houses came the sounds of washing up, and from the town centre, the church bell tolled. Seven o'clock.

At the head of the Enzweg, which from there follows the river below the town's back gardens, is a stone wall you can lean against to watch the water go past. It could have been my meal of *Maultaschen mit Felsenwein*, but perhaps it was the Enz itself that made me stand there staring into space, struggling to hold on to a single thought. It brought to mind something I heard a few months earlier from a woman in Düsseldorf, who confided in me that her soul and the river were inextricably linked. She had been seriously ill for some time, so ill in fact that she had, as it were, stood on the riverbank waiting for the proverbial ferryman. But she survived, because the Rhine had lifted her soul and given her hope, had made her realise she had to let everything go, that the river would flush away all that darkness if she would just let it. It took years, but she persevered and it passed. No, those years were not lost, because she had shared them with the river. It understood her. And cured her.

Her husband was there when she told me this. He wore plaid trousers, and he said nothing. He had been there, too, when she was sick. And he, too, had been patient.

It had rained upstream and the murky water crashed, frothing, over the barriers. On the far bank, on the promontory where the ancillary stream branches off from the main one, a few tree trunks lay in the water. They had got stuck between the barrier and the riverbank. A man of around sixty, in a light-blue T-shirt and faded blue cap, was trying to prise one of them loose with a long pole. Before I knew it, I had stood there watching for a quarter of an hour. And the man had been at it all that time. The trunk would shift a bit, but then fall back.

The headwaters of the Enz and its tributary the Nagold meander along wooded slopes. Occasionally a tree trunk glides into the water and embarks on a long journey downstream to Besigheim. They tend to get stuck in low-hanging branches, river bends, and barriers or weirs. There they wait, sometimes for years, until heavy rainfall makes the water rise, then they come loose and continue on their journey, turning slowly as they go. By the time they reach Besigheim they've lost all their leaves, their roots have been rinsed clean of forest earth, and algae grows on their bark.

This was the state of the trunk across the river, although it still had some branches, which gave it a bit of tired traction as the man attempted to dislodge it. Was he a descendant of the nail manufacturer? Yet another Ernst Conrad or Wilhelm, for whom the memory of the undoing of the business, a family drama, was still fresh? Or was he a former employee whose job it was, when the factory was still in operation, to keep the waters to the power station clear of floating debris?

Whoever he was, he stoically kept at it, changing poles, attacking the tree trunk from one angle and then from another. He showed no sign whatsoever of impatience, despair or frustration. Insignificant but patient, he wrestled with the river. Like a village schoolboy trying to get to grips with a too-difficult assignment, but persevering because he's sure there is an answer.

He lives in the assurance, I imagine, that with perseverance and faith, the day will come when all comes right.

ANCHORS AWEIGH

Canals are dull.

Christiaan Boogaard, Rhine skipper

The *Terra Maris* moors at the Nouryon salt plant in Delfzijl on the night of 15 April 2019. While a tall metal chute on the quay positions itself over the open cargo hold of the 110-metre barge, her skipper, Christiaan Boogaard, checks his computer one last time for the expected water levels along the Rhine. Even though Delfzijl's Oosterhornhaven is still far from the catchment area, the river begins here, right where the barge is being loaded. The *Terra Maris* arrived empty. Sitting high above the water line, she had cruised up the Ems Canal, straight through East Groningen, the wheelhouse lowered like a head sunk between the shoulders. Wide vistas stretched out on both sides. Lapwings tumbled above the farmland, herons glided above the reed-lined shores. The world passed by slowly, an unhurried landscape.

But now, night has fallen, the view has dissolved into darkness, and the lights of the chemical factory shine eerily on the *Terra Maris*. Once she is fully loaded and sails out into the river basin, the vessel will lie deeper in the water and the wheelhouse can be raised again. It's more comfortable for the skipper if the ceiling isn't pressing down on his neck.

The chute shudders and begins to disgorge salt, harvested from deep under the East Groningen soil. In the hold, the salt gradually collects into a cone-shaped heap. On one of the many softly lit displays in the wheelhouse, you can see how the ship's bow starts to dip downward, ever so slowly.

Christiaan consults the website for the expected water depth at the Kaub gauging station in the Rhine Gorge – "the mountains," he calls it – because he needs to know how far above the shallowest point in his journey to Mainz the water will be in five days' time. Understanding the gauging system (the measurement is called a *Pegel* in German) requires a degree of know-how. If the forecast for Kaub is a water level of 133, this does not mean the Rhine is 133 centimetres deep. At the Kaub gauging station, as every Rhine captain knows, you can add a metre to the level when calculating the maximum draught. That's a safe approximation, but there are some skippers who add 115 centimetres, scraping through with a draught of nearly two and a half metres.

"That's for the daredevils," Christiaan says.

His own rule of thumb is to maintain a margin of twenty centimetres extra depth, more than a hand's breadth below the keel. And, if there's strong wind, enough freeboard for when they're on the IJsselmeer, where things can get hairy, especially just past the Rotterdamse Hoek, a notoriously dangerous bend in the Noordoostpolder dyke.

Now he checks the weather forecast. It's also important to know if there's been rain upstream on tributaries like the Neckar, the Moselle or the Main. If that water flows into the Rhine, it can mean a difference of up to a metre in water levels. But if it hasn't rained, there's simply not much water. Wary of the rocky bottom at Trechtingshausen, just upstream of Kaub, Christiaan decides to load no more than the agreed 1,632 tons, not even two-thirds of his cargo capacity. On the bank of Trechtingshausen is St Clement's Chapel, where Rhinefarers used to stop to thank God for safe passage through the mountains.

Once the first salt cone has been loaded, the chute shifts back a bit and starts pouring the second one. The *Terra Maris* slowly rights herself.

When I wake up the next morning – it's still dark, the full red moon in the western sky – we're out on the IJsselmeer. The skipper's wife, Anna, and the Latvian crewman, Ruslans, are still fast asleep. She below deck, he in his cabin way up at the bow of the ship. Christiaan is in the wheelhouse. He looks out over the glistening surface, reddish silver against black. To the right, there's open water. The beam from the Urk lighthouse shines obliquely over to the port side.

I look out across the water and fall back to sleep.

A few hours later, Anna takes over in the wheelhouse so Christiaan can catch forty winks. The *Terra Maris* is approaching Amsterdam and it's busy on the water. Ships from Lelystad and Enkhuizen, pleasure boats, everything sails into the funnel of the Outer IJ, where one passes through the busy Schellingwoude lock and around a bend to the Amsterdam–Rhine Canal.

As we leave the lock, the voice of a female traffic controller comes through the marine VHF radio. The bend is difficult to survey and all manner of barges, work vessels, yachts, sloops and sports fishermen criss-cross the water. Anna manoeuvres her way through the throng, muttering under her breath. She comes from a long line of bargees. Her children attend a boarding school for skippers' children in Dordrecht. She went to the same school back in the day, before training to be a medical secretary. Her classmates at boarding school felt like family. That bond is for life. "It's hard to imagine if you haven't experienced it yourself."

Christiaan reappears just before we reach Utrecht. He had risen at 4 a.m. to start sailing and has now grabbed a few hours' sleep. "You've got to be able to function on little sleep in this job," he says. "You can only switch off once you're there."

We drink coffee and watch the slow-moving banks. Occasionally Christiaan comments on a house we're passing. He knows every brick, every washing line, every garden gate, every bench and nearly every barge he passes. If he and the other skipper are acquainted, they have a brief chat on channel 77. About where from and where to, but also about shipping companies, stevedores, cooperatives, about their children, about things that have happened, or are about to. And that they hope to cross paths again soon. And then the ships have passed each other and only their bow waves collide.

"Canals are dull," Christiaan says as we emerge from the sluice at Wijk bij Duurstede and cross the uppermost branch of the Rhine, which to port is called the Nether Rhine and to starboard the Lek. The three weirs spread over the Lek regulate the current and water levels, so that upstream the water will choose to flow into the IJssel rather than the Nether Rhine. A glance to the left, a glance to the right, and the *Terra Maris* resumes her journey between perfectly straight, artificial banks.

"There's no life in a canal," Christiaan continues. "It's dead water."

I wonder out loud if his vocation is mentioned in the Bible. So between Ravenswaaij and Tiel we – two Protestant guys transporting 1,632 tons of salt, bracing ourselves for the headstrong river – try to come up with boatsmen, harbours and rivers in the Old and New Testaments. It's a pretty unsuccessful quest for water in the story of a desert folk. We talk about Noah, the skipper of the Great Flood; about the fishermen on the Sea of Galilee; about St Paul's shipwreck; about Jonah, who was thrown overboard to calm the storm. Solomon had cedars shipped from Lebanon; the king of Tyre, fancying himself Neptune, had a palace on the sea. It's slim pickings. Rivers are few and far between in the holy scriptures: the Nile, the Jordan, the Euphrates, the Tigris, and that's about it.

Christiaan hesitates, then strays into the world of Scriptural commentary. Asks if I'd heard of "Death's Jordan", which Protestant preachers invoke in times of hardship. It is the Calvinists' River Styx, which somewhere in the spiritual world blocks our way to the other side, the End, Death. One day, as we all know, we will have to cross it.

There the conversation ends, because up ahead is the sluice at Tiel. And just beyond that, the Waal.

"Just one more lock, and then we'll sail for real," Christiaan says.

On the other side of the lock, it's a whole different world. The canal widens into a basin where ships can position themselves before continuing downriver. And that river is a wild animal. Ships heading downstream glide by, but the *Terra Maris* must sail upstream, so she has to cross to the south bank.

Going downstream is a breeze; upstream is a struggle. While a traffic regulator recites the names of the various vessels heading up- or downstream, the *Terra Maris* man-oeuvres her bow against the current. An empty ship, the *Crescendo*, passes, followed by a double barge carrying three tiers of containers. From the opposite direction, a passenger ship comes barrelling nearer.

"We're going to step on it," Christiaan says. He pushes a handle forwards, the engine revs audibly and the *Terra Maris* speeds up. "Check out the speed," he says.

I see that the *Terra Maris*, picking up pace, will hit 14 kilometres per hour. Christiaan nods to starboard. "I'm going a lot faster than that barge, anyway."

We steam up against the untamed current, which takes hold of the ship, jostles and gently shakes her. The engine growls, the ship vibrates. Christiaan, now standing spread-legged, draws my attention to the speedometer. The current is pushing us back, from 14 to 11 kilometres per hour.

"At times like these, you really learn to respect your engine," he says. "You need each other."

The force of the river shudders through the ship. Whichever way I look, it's hectic on the river. The *Crescendo* suddenly changes course, nips into a gap between a passing Viking cruise ship (where did *that* suddenly come from?) and, before I know it, a tugboat has passed us downstream.

"And you can keep track of all this?" I ask.

"*This* is the river," he says. "It's alive."

"So the river is a person?"

"Mister Writer," he laughs. He's having a bit of fun with me. And then, "Yes, he's a person."

"A 'he,' then?"

"Yes, a 'he'."

He doesn't say so, but it's clear: sailing upstream, against the current, isn't for wimps. It's a test of strength, a struggle. If the engine cuts out, you're done for.

I can sail with them as far as Cologne, a two-day journey. Before the city emerges from the darkness on either side of the river, like a brightly lit stone-and-glass jungle, we pass a wooded eastern shoreline where, here and there, small clusters of people huddle around campfires. Their faces are dimly lit, sparks rise from their midst.

Opposite, on the west bank, are houses. This is what it looked like, I imagine, when the Romans designated the river as a border. Darkness dotted with fires on the east bank, settlements and forts on the west. Even now, the region's oldest cities, from Mainz to Nijmegen, are on the Roman side of the Rhine.

Before we reach the quay, just beyond the church of St Martin, deckhand Ruslans drops anchor and the *Terra Maris* comes to rest for the night. I'll sleep on the ship and debark early tomorrow morning.

On the rear deck, Christiaan and Anna open a bottle of wine and we talk about the river, about the sailing life, about Anna's father's barge that crawled its way against the current between St Goar and Bingen, about high water due to snowmelt, and the predictability of the seasons. About how that is vanishing. The Rhine is changing from a glacial river back into the rainfall river it was three million years ago. With all the unpredictability that goes with it.

"Last October, the water was so low we almost couldn't sail," Christiaan says. "The Kaub reading was twenty-eight." He looks at me to see if it's sunk in. "Twenty-eight!" he repeats.

I recall that with the Kaub measurements, you have to add a metre to calculate the depth of the shallows. "One metre twenty-eight, then," I say. And I hold my hand at about chest height. "But what's your ship's draught?"

"Aft, it's a good metre and a half. When she's empty."

"So you couldn't sail," I say.

"We loaded 457 tons, just two little heaps in the hold,"

Christiaan says, showing me a photo on his phone. "Not right in the middle of the ship, but slightly forward, you see? So that the stern lies a bit higher in the water, like a seesaw. We just cleared it. But we had to have a guaranteed load for the return trip, because with an empty hold we wouldn't have made it home."

"So you took on a small cargo so as to lie shallower?"

Christiaan nods. He scrolls to another photo on his phone. "Check this out," he says. "In Bingen the water was so low we could actually walk to the Mouse Tower. Usually you can only get there by boat."

"And in Worms you could see the bottom," Anna adds.

"From the bow," Christiaan says. He points towards the front, where almost a hundred metres further up, the *Terra Maris* is anchored.

"On all sides," Anna corrects him. "From here on the bridge, too." She points to the balcony next to the wheel-house. "You could see the stones lying on the bottom. It was that shallow, and clear."

"That's because it hadn't rained for so long," says Christiaan. "When it rains, especially on the tributaries, and washes the river, then you have brown propeller wash. But this was crystal clear."

"We spoke to an Upper Rhine pilot," Anna says. "In sixty-five years he hadn't seen anything like it."

"What did the bottom look like?"

"Just pebbly," Christiaan says.

We drink. Upstream from Kaub, I marvel, you could just wade across the Rhine. You could see where you were stepping.

"So you weren't short of work?"

"Cargo space was in such demand that we were booked

three trips ahead," says Christiaan. "With high water, this can be a cut-throat business, but that year every barge was in service."

"So the river's changing," I say.

After a while, Anna replies, "And it stays the same, too."

∗

A year and a half later, in early September, I get a call from Christiaan saying that the *Terra Maris* is in Aschaffenburg, on the Main, and that I can sail back to Rotterdam with them if I like.

The next day I walk along the harbourside and see the barge moored on the quay. Two cranes take turns dropping grabberfuls of scrap metal into the *Terra Maris* hold. The ship smells of rust. With every clawful of scrap that falls into the hold, she shudders a bit.

Christiaan welcomes me aboard, and soon we're standing in the wheelhouse, watching the cargo hold fill up with discarded items.

"What's your favourite cargo?"

"Grain," Christiaan says without hesitation. "If you think about the hunger in the world, and that your hold is full of that precious stuff . . . it's fantastic. Like gold."

We watch as a grabber full of scrap metal hesitates above the hold, then lets go. Down tumble a radiator, a shopping-trolley chassis, a washing-machine drum, a broken cable, a silencer, a driveshaft, part of a pump, a lid, a chunk from a rubbish skip, a grate.

"With scrap metal, you're actually carrying a shipful of stories," Christiaan says.

∗

The next day, sometime after noon, the *Terra Maris* is loaded and sets off up the Main. The river is lazy: dozens of weirs have tamed the water. The ship makes her way comfortably from lock to lock. Tomorrow is Friday, and at nine in the morning the children arrive in Duisburg by train from Dordrecht. Christiaan does his calculations: if he can catch the last sluice tonight and sail into the Rhine at 4 a.m., he'll have just enough time.

The Main is well-nigh empty. The trees lining the banks are still in full late-summer foliage. It has rained a lot in the past few days and a bubble of water is heading from all corners of the catchment area towards the Rhine. The Kaub prediction is around 240. Christiaan has a load of 2,189 tons, the *Terra Maris*' draught is a tad more than 280 centimetres.

Upstream along the Main, in the other direction, is the canal that leads to the Danube, to the other Europe. But even though that route is wide open, ships rarely travel from the east towards the Rhine. The canal is still new, but the division is millions of years old.

"They're just different," says Anna, who has joined us on the bridge.

There's still rain in the air. Swallows glide low over the water, wagtails land on the ship and take off again towards the far shore. Where the trees thin out along the bank, there are benches where people sit watching the ships pass. The *Terra Maris* has to go through seven sluices, and from the bridges over those sluices, cyclists stop and look down at the scrap metal. Someone points, another waves.

In Frankfurt, the working day is over and young people's voices resonate across the water. Paddleboards, kayaks, scullers, a lone party boat. Flats glide past on the starboard side.

Christiaan moors at midnight. He's missed the last lock, so will have to push off again at half past two. The engine falls silent, sleep descends upon the ship.

It's 4 a.m. and still dark when the *Terra Maris* reaches the Rhine. She sails out of the mouth of the Main, and the only indication that the current picks her up and carries her along is her speed and gentle, rocking calmness. Without any audible difference in the sound of the engine, we speed up from 11 to 14 kilometres per hour. Mainz glides past in the dark, its cathedral a mysterious shadow against the night sky.

As day breaks just before Bingen, and we pass the Mouse Tower and sail into mountain country, I notice that the buoys on either side are being pulled sideways by the current. It's as if the *Terra Maris* is being lifted from behind, and the water is simultaneously carrying us and pushing us down. We pick up speed, the mountains envelop us, sharp bends block our view upstream.

We've come through the valley of the Main where Einhard was born, in Mainz we passed the spot where Charlemagne rebuilt the Roman bridge, we've sailed alongside the island where Drogo stood at Louis the Pious' deathbed. And now that morning has broken and daylight is chasing the darkness from forests, vineyards, cliffs, picturesque hamlets, commuter trains, ferries and quays, I think of what's still ahead: the influx of the Moselle carrying Willibrord's holy droplets, the banks of Kaub, Remagen and Tolkamer, where military commanders led their troops across the water. We will pass Xanten, where the Romans rowed northwards in their triremes to subjugate the Chauci; we'll see where Ambiorix swam across the Rhine; and yes, we will round the rock of the Lorelei.

The water is still grey under the cloudy skies, while the wooded hillsides begin to take on some colour. From the banks come the sounds of church bells and locomotives.

Once we've passed the rock of the Lorelei, Christiaan retires for some sleep. Anna offers me a cup of coffee and takes over the wheel. She sees me looking out at the river.

"We had an elderly man on board once," she says. "He sat looking out from the aft deck, and I noticed he was crying. I went over and asked what was wrong. He said, 'All my life, I've seen pictures of the Rhine and the mountains and those little wood-timbered houses, and now I'm here, and I'm old.'"

We watch in silence, and the *Terra Maris* wends her way up the deep-water channel. Outside, in the open cargo hold, are 2,000 tons of scrap metal. We are a ship laden with stories, and a big, soft tide of rainwater has lifted us up and is carrying us to the sea.

And finally . . .

When I began work on this book, I expected to be able to portray the Rhine as an ancient yet mortal person. Its birth would coincide with the creation of the Alps, and its death with their erosion. I had hoped for a turbulent conception and a worthy death scene, bookends to an alternately stormy and sullen life amongst bank dwellers who by turns feared or embraced it.

But Kim Cohen soon put paid to that notion. He convinced me that the Rhine had always been there, even before the Alps rose from the sea, and that it'll still exist, in one form or another, after time and the elements have erased those accidental mountain ranges and new mountains have been pushed upwards, and new coasts will line new, as-yet-unnamed oceans.

If I had truly set out to describe the birth and death of the river, then my story should have stretched across billions of years, from Earth's first rainfall until its last. For the river is not the chance bed over which water babbles for everyone to see, it's the entire, tilted plate of sand and stone that carries the rainwater there. As long as it rains, there will be a river.

In the wonderful opening chapter of her book *Rain*, the American journalist Cynthia Barnett describes how the very first rain fell on Earth four billion years ago. In the sensual style of someone who experienced it first hand, she explains how our planet, during its first half billion years, was an 8000-degree inferno of churning molten rock that suffered a relentless bombardment of meteorites. "Time and again," she writes, "the young Earth built up a crust, only to see it incinerated by storms of flaming meteors."

Not water, but boulders were the first thing to come raining down on our planet. Like gigantic stone droplets, the meteorites burst open upon impact; the water they released vaporised, sought cooler, higher altitudes, and either swirled around there or disappeared back into the heavens.

"It hissed away into space," Barnett writes.

But when, after those first hellish half billion years, the meteorite showers waned and the Earth's surface finally got the chance to cool off into a crust, that kilometres-thick cloud cover was able to sink downwards.

"As the last of the flaming chunks fell to the surface or hurtled away, the planet finally had a chance to cool. The water vapour could condense.

"At long last, it began to rain."

This was the birth of the Earth's rivers: the first rainfall, the first brook gurgling away from the first overflowing rain puddle, the first droplets from a rocky overhang, the first wet slope in an otherwise lifeless world.

And should the rivers, *Deo volente*, not be yanked out of existence along with us by some cosmic cataclysm or other, but rather die of old age, then they still have at least five billion years to go, until the sun runs out of steam, swells up, explodes, and all the water and all the rock gets catapulted back to where it came from, into the infinity of space.

*

This is what geology does to me: it makes me feel small and arbitrary, and – like Jacobus Thijsse said in his book *Our Great Rivers* – surprised by my surroundings. It's that encounter between paltry undertakings and the enormous, blind machinery of nature that I want to write about; the meeting of our blithe muddling with the slow-moving landscape in which we wander.

That's why this book, like my previous books *The Wadden Islands* and *Down Old Roads*, rambles through the no-man's-land between man and nature, imagination and science, fiction and non-fiction.

Talking to scientists and bank dwellers, reading articles and other sources, and travelling through the river basin brought me not only timeless knowledge, but an abundance of life; a sackful of wriggling creatures that I let out, one at a time, in stories.

Whether it is under Christiaan Boogaard's barge, around the deathbed of Louis the Pious, past the cannons of Bratge, above the salmon's eggs or underneath the poem about the girl of Rheinfelden: the river is always nearby; everywhere, the water of the Rhine flows with feigned indifference towards the sea.

Kim Cohen said that the Rhine was always there, and since I cannot dissociate myself from my own perspective as a blithe muddler who tries, and fails, to fathom the heartbeat of nature, I am humbly prepared to add to it that the Rhine will be there always, and will never die.

Acknowledgements

I wish to thank Pietro Biancardi, Christiaan and Anna Boogaard, Peter Boorsma, Dr Arjen V.A.J. Bosman (Military Legacy Dordrecht), Gert Karel Bruggert, Kim Cohen, Daniela and Erhard from Warnemünde (in case anyone knows their surname, which I forgot to ask: info@ overoudewegen.com), Ida de Muijnck-Deen, Henk Diependaal, Ad Dubbeldam, Wim Eikelboom, Karel Essink, Henny Groenendijk, Tom Hazeberg, Eeltsje Hettinga, Douwe van Hinsbergen, Bernt Kerremans, Hans Peter and Beatrice Kistler, Wim Klinkert, Dick Mol, Erik Nieuwenhuis, Lars Noorbergen, Luc Panhuijsen, Marian and Arno van der Pluijm, Thomas Rathgeber, Katja Reichenstein and Tom Brunner, Karin Sant, Kommer Tanis, Ed Thorogood and Hanneke Klep, Steven Van Ammel, Gerrit Vossebelt and Erwin Winter for their hospitality, tips, time, stories, generosity and expertise.

Thanks to P.J.M. Martens for his book *The Salmon Fishers of the Biesbosch*, from which I wholeheartedly drew for the segment on William of Orange's boat trip on the Verdronken Waard in 1560.

Thanks to my publisher, Arend Hosman, who asked me to write about the Rhine, and to editor Saartje Schwachöfer for encouragingly reading along with me, chapter by chapter. Thank you to Jasper Henderson, to whom Arend passed the torch at Thomas Rap and who embraced this project. My thanks to editor Roel van Diepen, who painstakingly got me and this book to the finish line. My gratitude to Anne Kramer, Nienke Beeking and all the otherwise unsung staff at the publishing house, who meticulously checked the manuscript for spelling, grammar and consistency, who saw to the layout, and who sent it into the world. I claim sole responsibility for the many stubborn peculiarities in the book, such as the incorrigible seaman's habit of referring to a ship as a woman.

And thanks to my beloved wife Kim, who read along with me, gave me the opportunity to travel and occasionally, together with our dog Blaffer, joined me on these excursions. Finally, thanks to my sons Midas and Joris, who climbed the Lorelei and leapt into the icy Posterior Rhine with me, and to my daughter Hannah, who gave, with my son(-in-law) Joe, an unforgettable party on the island of Vis, where this book began.

Translators' acknowledgements

The extract from the poem *Time* by M. Vasalis was translated by David McKay.

The lines from Petrarch's *Italia mia, benché 'l parlar sia indarno* (*Canzione 128*) were translated by A.S. Kline.

The extract from *The Ister* by Friedrich Hölderlin was translated by James Mitchell.

The lines from *Mosella* by Ausonius were translated by Hugh Gerard Evelyn White.

Extracts from Caesar's *The Gallic War* and Tacitus' *Annals* were adapted from the translations by Carolyn Hammond and J.C. Yardley respectively, slight changes being necessary to better reflect the Dutch text.

We are grateful to Susan Massotty for her translation of the first stanza of *Tusken twa seeën* by the Frisian poet Tsjêbbe Hettinga, and for allowing us to use extracts from her translation of Hettinga's poems *De mar* and *It faderpaard*.

All other translations are our own or are available in open-source documents.

The conclusions as to Charlemagne's actual height can be found in an article by Frank J. Rühli, Bernhard Blümich and Maciej Henneberg in *Economics & Human Biology*, Volume 8, Issue 2, July 2010.

For a fascinating short documentary about "The Robinson of the Rhine," go to https://vimeo.com/52925691

We would like to take this opportunity to thank the Dutch Foundation for Literature and Flanders Literature for their support during this project.

MATHIJS DEEN writes fiction, crime fiction and non-fiction, and also for radio. His book *Over Oude Wegen* ("Down Old Roads", 2018) was the winner of the Halewijn Prize, and has been widely translated. His crime novels, set among the west Frisian islands in the North Sea, are now bestsellers in Germany.

After a career as a translator at the Dutch foreign ministry, JANE HEDLEY-PRÔLE took up literary translation, specializing in Dutch and Flemish non-fiction. In her spare time she likes to play pool and travel by cargo ship.

Longtime Amsterdam resident JONATHAN REEDER translates contemporary Dutch and Flemish fiction and non-fiction as well as mid-20th-century classics. A former professional orchestra musician, he also translates opera libretti and essays on classical music.